ON THE RECORD

BY JOHN TOBLER

Interviews edited by Michael Smith
Track-by-track analysis by Robert M. Corich

BOOKS LTD

Photography courtesy of Pictorial Press

This edition published in Great Britain in 2011 by
Coda Books Ltd, The Barn, Cutlers Farm Business Centre, Edstone,
Wootton Wawen, Henley in Arden, Warwickshire, B95 6DJ
www.codabooks.com

Copyright © 2011 Coda Books Ltd

All rights reserved. No part of this publication may be reproduced or transmitted in any form or by any means, electronic or mechanical, including photocopy, recording, or any information storage and retrieval system, without permission in writing from the publisher.

A CIP catalogue record for this book is available from the British Library
ISBN: 978-1-906783-59-4

CONTENTS

ON THE RECORD 4
By John Tobler

IN THEIR OWN WORDS 83
Interviews with Anni-Frid and ABBA insiders
Edited by Michael Smith

TRACK-BY-TRACK ANALYSIS 128
By Robert M. Corich

"I had a dream and it was fulfilled by meeting with Benny, Bjorn and Agnetha."
ANNI-FRID LYNGSTAD

On the record

It all started for ABBA with the Eurovision Song Contest in 1974, which was held in Brighton on the south coast of England. Prior to that memorable day, ABBA were not completely unknown, as they had made some progress in their native Scandinavia, as well as in South Africa, Australia, Holland and Belgium. In fact, the group had even had a single, Ring Ring, released in Britain, although it had been far from a hit.

When their next single, Waterloo, had been selected as the Swedish entry for the 1974 Song Contest, the quartet, and especially their manager, Stig Anderson, resolved to do as much preparation for the Big Day as humanly possible. Anderson had canvassed the opinions of many music business professionals around Europe, and had been told that, because ballads had been successful in the previous few Eurovision events, there was a good chance that the next winner would be a more uptempo song.

With this in mind, Anderson, along with the two male members of ABBA, Benny Andersson (no relation – Benny's surname includes a double 's', while Stig's had only one) and Björn Ulvaeus, set about composing a song whose title would be instantly recognisable throughout Europe. They decided on Waterloo, which was the name of a famous one day battle in June, 1815, in which a British Army, led by the Duke Of Wellington and assisted by soldiers from several other continental European countries, defeated Napoleon Bonaparte's French Army. The day resulted in 50,000 soldiers (25% of all the soldiers in the Battle of Waterloo) being killed in a single day. The event was certainly hugely significant in European history of the early nineteenth century, and was indeed familiar to most educated Europeans, who might be persuaded to support a song about such an iconic subject.

With a bouncy tune and a title which was repeated frequently throughout the song and which could be easily pronounced throughout the world, the next thing was the lyrics, which ideally should reflect the subject matter suggested by the song title. In those early days, the lyrics were often suggested by Stig Anderson, but Björn, in particular, made huge strides as a lyricist during ABBA's active career of almost a decade as one of the biggest acts in the world, and by the time of the musical Chess, for which he and Benny wrote the music with Sir Tim Rice as lyricist, Rice noted that he and Björn had collaborated on some lyrics.

Björn's obvious problem was that English was not his native tongue, although there seem to be very few Swedes of ABBA's generation who have not learnt English as a second language at school, but as he travelled with the band, Björn's grasp of the English language improved considerably, assisted by the fact that he listened to innumerable British and American records. Stig, on the other hand, had served his musical apprenticeship first as a performer before moving into management, music publishing and eventually an entire record label. As he was somewhat older than the members of ABBA, who were born between 1945 and 1950, Anderson knew many pre-rock 'n' roll musical styles, while Benny and Björn grew up liking such 1960s acts as the Beatles and the Beach Boys, so that their lyrical perspective was relatively narrow compared to their manager who was very familiar with the music of the previous three decades, and great composers of popular music like George Gershwin, Cole Porter, Jerome Kern, Rodgers & Hammerstein, etc.

Bear in mind that Stig realised that to have a chance of Eurovision glory, ABBA would have to perform in English rather than Swedish because, without being xenophobic, it is impossible to sing rock 'n' roll in any other language than English. However, Stig could probably guess that this photogenic young quartet of two pretty girls who could both sing very well, and their musician boyfriends/fiancés, who had both served their time in domestically famous Swedish groups before establishing a potent songwriting partnership, were capable of the international big time. However, Stig (and Björn & Benny) had experienced rejection in both the previous two years with songs they had written for Eurovision.

In 1972, they had written Better To Have Loved for Lena Andersson, a Swedish vocalist said to be a cross between Joan Baez and Judy Collins, but when Ms Andersson performed it in the Swedish Eurovision heat it was placed third, although it was also released as a single in Sweden and topped the Swedish chart.

By 1973, Benny and Björn had written a song on which Anni-Frid and Agnetha appeared along with them. This was People Need Love, and at first Stig Anderson refused to credit the girls on the record label, reasoning that using the name Björn, Benny, Agnetha and Frida was too long for people to remember, especially as the track was to be released in the US, where it had been licensed to the Playboy label, which was connected with the world famous magazine of the same name. The compromise for the American release was that the single was released as by Björn & Benny with Svenska Flicka, which apparently means 'Swedish girl', although for the domestic Swedish release, the artist credit was to Björn & Benny, Agnetha & Anni-Frid. Interestingly, People Need Love was bubbling under the Top 100 of the US singles chart when Playboy Records began to experience major problems with distribution of the single, which made it impossible for it to continue to climb the chart past Number 115, although this was apparently the highest position ever achieved in the US chart by a Swedish record at that time.

A follow-up single, He Is Your Brother, was also successful, and, at the end of 1972, the Swedish Broadcasting Company approached Björn, Benny and Stig, inviting them to write a song for the Swedish heat of Eurovision 1973, even though Better to Have Loved had been rejected for the 1972 contest. Stig Anderson in particular was well aware that for his group to appear in Eurovision would guarantee them massive exposure all over Europe, especially in Britain, which was the musical gateway to the rest of the world. The song was very important, and at the start of the year, Benny & Björn worked hard on the music, which they intended to sound like a peal of bells, while Stig wrote the lyrics to Ring Ring.

Not everything went as planned. Agnetha was pregnant and the predicted birth date was in the same week as the Swedish heat, but Elin Linda, Björn & Agnetha's first child, wasn't born until nearly two weeks after the heat, so Agnetha was able to perform with Björn, Benny and Anni-Frid. By all accounts, they were streets ahead of the competition, but the problem was that the decision about which song should represent Sweden in Eurovision was made by a panel of so-called musical experts, who clearly failed to take into account the audience reaction to Ring Ring, and placed the song third, the same position as the previous year's Better to Have Loved. The whole affair became a national scandal, and public opinion forced a change for

The group after their Eurovision win in 1974

future Swedish Eurovision heats, when the audience and the general public would decide who would represent Sweden. Without this enforced alteration, the story of ABBA might be quite different, although there is little doubt that the rest of the world would have eventually discovered the quartet without Eurovision.

Even though it was not chosen for Eurovision 1973, Ring Ring was a massive success.

By this time, ABBA were recording new songs in both Swedish and English, and the Swedish language version of the song topped the charts in Denmark, Finland and Norway as well as Sweden, where the English language version was at Number 2 in the chart behind the Swedish version, with the Ring Ring LP at Number 3. The English version was also Number 1 in South Africa, Australia, Holland and Belgium, as already mentioned.

The result of all this success was that Stig Anderson found himself being interviewed by seemingly the entire Swedish media – radio, newspapers and magazines, TV – and because he found himself having to say Björn & Benny, Anni-Frid and Agnetha very frequently, devised the acronym by which ABBA were (and are) known, which has served them very well. Interestingly, the name ABBA had been used in the music industry prior to the Swedish quartet's emergence. Just after the end of World War II, a songwriter named Eden Ahbez (who believed that only Gods deserved to have their names spelt with capital letters) wrote a song titled Nature Boy, which was the first US Number 1 hit for Nat 'King' Cole in 1948, and Mr Ahbez was known as Abba. A decade and a half later few remembered the name, although, initially, there was some concern that the name was also that of a Swedish company which sold canned fish, whose directors were worried lest ABBA the quartet should bring the name into disrepute, but after Stig Anderson had assured them that ABBA were aiming to publicise the name in a very positive way, the concern abated. It hadn't been so easy in 1973, when Stig Anderson attempted to get Ring Ring released in Britain, but was initially turned down by several labels. Eventually, Epic, a part of the CBS/Columbia organisation, signed them for that single, but only after the lyrics to the English language version had been re-written by Neil Sedaka & Phil Cody, his writing partner of the time. Sedaka, an American singer/songwriter/pianist, accumulated 29 US hits as an artist between 1958 and 1977, including three Number Ones, and wrote most, if not all, his own material. He even wrote Is This the Way to Amarillo, but we won't hold that against him… Despite this enviable track record, the Sedaka/Cody lyrics seem nothing special, and when the single appeared in Britain in 1973 it was almost totally ignored. Ring Ring was not an auspicious start to the career of an act who can only be described as international superstars.

Interestingly, Ring Ring became one of the first ABBA songs to be covered, which it was by an Irish group called The Others, whose version made the local Top 20. The flip side of Ring Ring, a song written by Björn and Benny without help from anyone else, titled Rock'n'Roll Band, was for some reason unavailable on a British CD by ABBA until the early 1990s.

Even though they knew they had to write and record a song for Eurovision 1974, the members of ABBA were busy during the summer of 1973, performing on a tour of venues in Sweden which are known as 'folk parks', for which they had been booked for some time, and rather than make excuses and cancel the gigs, the quartet decided to use the live work as a kind of rehearsal for the Eurovision Contest, which was only months away.

We all know that Waterloo was the launch pad for ABBA, but there were two other contenders before the decision was made to use Waterloo; Stig was going on about the title 'Honey Pie' for a while, before realising that Waterloo was a much better concept, while Björn and Benny came up with the tune for Hasta Mañana, but this was a song which chiefly featured Agnetha, whereas the song used should involve all members of the quartet equally, so it was Waterloo that was chosen.

The next decision involved the visual aspects of the performance and, although it is hard in 2006 to mention his name in polite conversation, the role model on which ABBA based their look for Eurovision was Gary Glitter, who at the time was one of the biggest stars in the British pop firmament, although in musical terms, many may find it hard to understand why. Thus ABBA's clothes were festooned with sequins, while Björn would be using a new guitar with a body shaped like a star, but many felt that the master stroke was having Sven-Olof Waldoff, who would be conducting the orchestra behind ABBA, wear an instantly recognisable Napoleon-styled hat. Even before the contest, Waterloo was released as a single in Sweden, and sold over 100,000 copies, while an album also titled Waterloo sold nearly as many.

Arriving in Brighton a few days before the contest, ABBA were supposedly favourites to win, but the day before the event, Olivia Newton-John, who was representing England with Long Live Love, had become the one to beat, while the Dutch duo, Mouth & McNeal, whose song was I See a Star, were also strongly fancied. Eventually, Mouth & McNeal were placed third, while second place went to Italian star Gigliola Cinquetti, who shared the spotlight with ABBA and others on what must be one of the rarest ABBA record releases. This was an EP titled The Music People at Eurovision, which included Waterloo by ABBA, Si by Gigliola Cinquetti, who was representing Italy, the previous year's Eurovision winner, Anne-Marie David's Wonderful Dream, and lastly Mein Ruf Nach Dir, sung by a lady bricklayer from Switzerland named Piera Martell, which was the Swiss Eurovision entry. Without much doubt, the only thing some of these artists had in common was that they were all signed to 'The Music People', as CBS Records referred to themselves at that time. Eventually both Olivia Newton-John, who came fourth, and Piera Martell were also-rans, while Gigliola Cinquetti probably wasn't heartbroken – she had already won Eurovision ten years before with Non Ho L'Eta Per Amarti, which was a UK Top 20 single, and she would re-record Si with English lyrics and the title Go (Before You Break My Heart), which reached the UK Top 10 soon after Eurovision.

On the night, there was only one possible winner. ABBA looked great (well, for 1974, they looked very exotic, which was in tune with the times of glam rock stars like Marc Bolan, David Bowie, Roy Wood & Wizzard, The Sweet, Mud, Slade and all the rest) and after a perfect performance of Waterloo, the audience went ape, and the various judges voted ABBA the winners of the 1974 Eurovision Song Contest, which some say was never the same after ABBA, by which they must surely mean that ABBA improved Eurovision, which was undoubtedly true. They were also the first Swedish act to win Eurovision. Whether Lordi, who won the 2006 Eurovision Song Contest with their extraordinary song, Hard Rock Hallelujah, becoming the first act representing Finland to win the contest, will also follow ABBA in dominating European charts for years to come, is uncertain, but this bizarre group who looked like refugees from Lord of the Rings had, like ABBA, spent time and trouble on their visual appearance as well as performing a reasonable song.

So that was the story of Waterloo, which topped the British singles chart for two weeks in May during a nine week spell in the chart. It also topped the singles chart in more than a dozen other countries, although perhaps the most significant achievement apart from topping the British chart was that the single also made the US Top 10, which was a huge bonus, as it was almost certainly true that ABBA's next ambition after winning Eurovision and topping the UK chart was to make an impression in the biggest market in the world, the USA. Hindsight tells us that this was one aim which failed to materialise for ABBA, although some would say it wasn't for lack of trying.

Of course, each of the four members of ABBA had been recording for some years before they convened to become a group. The first of the quartet to appear was Björn Christian Ulvaeus, who was born on 25 April 1945, near Gothenburg, in the south of Sweden, but moved with his parents as a child to Vastervik, a town on the east coast of Sweden, some way south of Stockholm, which also produced a world beating tennis star of the 1990s in Stefan Edberg.

Björn asked for and was given his first guitar for his thirteenth birthday, when he had expressed interest in playing an instrument after hearing skiffle

Abba performing on TV in the early seventies dressed in Christmas fayre

music on the radio, and his early attempts at playing were in the skiffle style popularised in Britain during the second half of the 1950s by Lonnie Donegan, after which the teenager followed the next British popular music trend, traditional jazz, also learning to play banjo, an instrument more often used in Dixieland jazz, as the style is also known, than guitar.

According to the breathtaking biography of the group, Bright Lights, Dark Shadows – The Real Story of ABBA, by Swedish author Carl Magnus Palm (Omnibus Press, 2001), which is far more insightful and accurate than all previous biographies of the group put together, as Palm had known ABBA for some time as a local journalist, the first band of which Björn was a member was known as the Partners. Their music had moved on from skiffle to the somewhat ersatz folk music of the Kingston Trio, who were probably the most popular American act during the period when Elvis Presley was in the US Army (the two years from March 1958, to March 1960). Five separate LPs by the Kingston Trio topped the US album chart for a total of 46 weeks in the two years from November, 1958, and they were incredibly successful during that period, although relatively few of their 17 US hit singles were hits in Europe, with the notable exception of their million-selling 1958 debut hit, Tom Dooley, which, incidentally, was the subject of a cover version in Britain by the aforementioned Lonnie Donegan, whose version just outsold the Kingston Trio original, although both were Top 5 hits.

Then came the kind of dilemma which has affected groups since the concept of groups was invented – another group also called the Partners had achieved some local success, and had been using the name longer than the Partners which included Björn, so another name had to be found by Björn and his colleagues, who decided to change their group name to the West Bay Singers – "West Bay" is the English translation of Vastervik, the place where the group was based. In the summer of 1963, the West Bay Singers went on a six week European tour in a Volvo – what else? - and got to Spain, where they tightened up their live act and grew in confidence.

In the autumn of 1963, Björn's mother heard about a radio talent contest and encouraged her son to enter the group in the competition. Stig Anderson's partner in his company, Polar Music, was a well-known talent scout with a good track record named Bengt Bernhag, who decided, in classic music industry style, that because the overwhelming fashion at the time in

Sweden was for bands to copy British and American beat group hits and sing in English, that an almost diagonally opposite approach would at least create publicity. He read about the talent contest, noted that the West Bay Singers had been praised, and felt they might be the act to sing folk songs in Swedish. In the wake of the Kingston Trio's success, a movement had arisen in the USA for hootenannies, these being gatherings at folk clubs where both audience and artists would be involved. So Bernhag decided to rename the West Bay Singers as the Hootenanny Singers, and the band became the first act to sign with Polar Music. They achieved considerable fame, with a string of hit singles between 1964 and 1966, but then the Swedish equivalent of Uncle Sam insisted that the group, apart from its German member, singer/guitarist Hansi Schwarz, must do their obligatory year of military training, which they had been delaying because they were so successful. On the night of their farewell show before their year in uniform, the Hootenanny Singers threw a party to which they invited their main rivals as Sweden's most popular act of the time, the Hep Stars, one member of which was a young keyboard player named Benny Andersson.

ABBA are all presumed to be of Swedish nationality, but, in fact, Anni-Frid Synni Lyngstad, whose date of birth is 15 November 1945, was actually born in Norway. Her mother, Synni Lyngstad, was the youngest child of a family who lived in Narvik, a town which had been captured by the German Army when Synni was 13 years old. The people of Narvik learned to live with the German occupation, which lasted around five years during the Second World War, and it is probably true to say that although any place eventually becomes used to seeing and living with an occupying force, they are usually unhappy that foreigners are telling them what to do. Synni had grown into a very attractive young lady by 1945, and she fell in love with a German soldier named Alfred Haase, and before long was pregnant with his child. For a young Norwegian girl to have fallen in love with a German was regarded as scandalous by the people of Narvik. At the end of the war, Haase returned to Germany, but before he left, apparently told Synni that he would return to Norway as soon as he could. However, when nothing happened for two years, Synni fell into a deep depression from which she died when she was 21, leaving the two-year-old Anni-Frid an orphan.

Fortunately, Synni's mother was not prepared to see her granddaughter suffer, and due to the anti-German feelings which were growing stronger in Narvik as the war came to a close, decided that the best thing she could do was to leave Narvik and attempt to start a new life with her granddaughter in a place where no one knew anything about her and her family. She decided to move to Sweden, and worked as a seamstress to provide for herself and Anni-Frid, eventually settling in Eskilstuna, a town to the west of Stockholm. Her grandmother encouraged Anni-Frid to sing from an early age, teaching her traditional Scandinavian folk songs, and this led to the pre-teen girl singing in public, where her talent was quickly noticed; by the time she was 13, she was singing with a dance band who performed in a restaurant in Eskilstuna, although she had to lie about her age, as she was three years too young to be

An early picture of the group at a publicity shoot

legally singing in public.

Still a teenager, she started singing jazz with a big band led by Bengt Sandlund. The bass player with that band was Ragnar Frederiksson, and Anni-Frid and Frederiksson launched their own band, The Anni-Frid Four, which became a big attraction in Eskilstuna. At the same time, she and Ragnar became lovers and eventually married, producing two children – Hans (born 1963) and Liselotte (born 1967) – but this was not enough for Anni-Frid, who had ambitions to make it by herself as a vocalist. One possible way of achieving this was for her to enter talent contests, first locally, which she invariably won, and then nationally, in a competition titled 'New Faces'. Part of the prize for this was that she would appear on television, and shortly before her twenty-second birthday, she was first seen on the small screen. It was a day that many people in Sweden would remember vividly, although not for that reason. On 3 September 1967, traffic in Sweden began to drive on the right hand side of the road, having previously driven on the left as in Britain.

Anni-Frid soon became a rising star of the Swedish music scene, and left Eskilstuna to live in Stockholm where she was at the centre of the local music industry, and signed with the local EMI label, for which she made a series of singles and an album, although none were hits, which was a disappointment to everyone involved. However, Anni-Frid was still an attraction for her live performances, often of well-known standards which she interpreted very well, although these were of little interest on record, where other artists had classic versions of songs by George Gershwin, Cole Porter, etc., easily available.

Nothing appeared to be going right for Anni-Frid, who had left her two children to be looked after by Ragnar after the inevitable divorce. It is probably impossible for a married couple to remain married for very long with such a distance between them. However, Anni-Frid justified her actions by saying that she knew her children would have a safer and happier upbringing in Eskilstuna with Ragnar than they would living with her in Stockholm as she attempted to further her career ambitions. She also vowed that she would never lose touch with Hans and Liselotte.

Then things began to improve for Anni-Frid in early 1969, when she was offered and accepted the offer of cabaret work with a veteran entertainer named Charlie Norman, who was very well respected in Sweden and performed all over the country. Had Anni-Frid attempted to also be a mother to her children as well as working with Norman, life would have been completely impossible and far worse than merely living in Stockholm, as Norman tended to work in monthly residencies, and she could have been away from home for months at a time.

Later in 1969, Anni-Frid and Charlie Norman were performing at a venue in Malmo, a place in the extreme south of Sweden, very close to Denmark, and by chance, the Hep Stars, with their dynamic young keyboard player Benny Andersson, were also performing that night in Malmo. This was at a time when the usual Hep Stars guitarist was absent from the group, and Benny's friend, Björn Ulvaeus, from the Hootenanny Singers, was deputising. Björn, Benny and Anni-Frid (with Charlie Norman) by chance all found themselves in the same restaurant after the shows had finished, and spent most of the night talking about music and getting to know each other.

Goran Bror "Benny" Andersson was born in a suburb of Stockholm on 16 December 1946. Not only his father, but also his paternal grandfather, enjoyed making music, and from the age of six, when he was given his first musical instrument, an accordion, Benny was quite obviously fascinated by the possibility of making music. With his father and grandfather, Benny was involved in his first group, which was known, due to the youth and promise of its youngest member, as Benny's Trio. According to Carl Magnus Palm's book, his stage debut, at Stockholm City Hall, came when he was only eight years old, and two years later, he was selected to be the leading child actor in a children's play. Also when he was ten, his parents presented him with his first piano, which was probably what Benny wanted more than anything else in the world at that time, but he claimed to learn far more about how to play the instrument from his grandfather than from formal lessons, which he apparently found tedious.

During the second half of the 1950s, Benny Andersson purchased his first records. The very first was by Caterina Valente, who was born in Paris to Italian parents, and was notable for the fact that she could supposedly sing in six languages. The single which attracted Benny sufficiently that he had to own a copy was titled You Are Music, although Ms Valente's biggest hit came in 1955 with her vocal version of Andalucia by the Cuban composer Ernesto Lecuona, to which lyrics in English were added in 1940 by Al Stillman. When Caterina Valente recorded it, the title of the song was The Breeze and I, and the single, which eventually sold a million copies, was a Top 10 hit in both Britain and the USA. The Book of Golden Discs by Joseph Murrells (Barrie & Jenkins, 1978) notes that Caterina 'was immersed in the art of entertainment from birth, her mother Maria acknowledged by many to be the most gifted clown in the world and billed as 'The Female Grock', her father, known as Di Zazzo, was a famed accordion virtuoso, and one of her brothers had mastery of 33 musical instruments. Her diverse background enabled her to interpret lyrics with equal facility in English, Spanish, French, Italian, German and Swedish'. Ms Valente retired from her career as an international celebrity and entertainer at the age of 72 in 2003, and she probably won't mind everyone knowing how old she is as long as we wish her a very long and pleasant retirement.

The second record that Benny acquired was Jailhouse Rock by Elvis Presley, which was a massive hit in late 1957, just before Presley was drafted and allowed the Kingston Trio to dominate the US charts (see above). If Benny had merely appreciated the artistic talent of Caterina Valente, rock 'n' roll was a very different ball game, and like teenagers all over the Western world, Benny was captivated by this wild and exciting music. He soon became recognised as a mover and shaker among his local contemporaries, not least because he was an excellent piano player.

Around this time, at the age of 15, he became seriously involved with a 17 year old girl named Christina Gronvall, whom he sometimes accompanied when she sang in theatrical productions. She and Benny became very close, and when Christina discovered she was pregnant, they announced that they were engaged, and in August 1963 they became the parents of a son named Peter. For Benny, becoming a father at the age of only 16 must have been a traumatic experience, but as he has always been a fairly relaxed person, he probably took it in his stride. Benny and Christina also produced another child, Helene, who was born on 25 June 1965.

In early 1964, he and Christina joined a band together, he as keyboard player, she as one of the two vocalists. The band was known as Elverkets Spelmanslag, and as well as normal bookings, they entered talent contests, in one of which they competed against the Hep Stars, and Benny's brilliance as a keyboard player was noticed by the Hep Stars, who were becoming popular, but were existing on very little money. In order to boost their income, lead singer Svenne Hedlund would from time to time allow others to hire his van, and when Elverkets Spelmanslag found themselves without transport but with a gig to play, they contacted Hedlund, who drove them to their show, and afterwards back to their homes. Hedlund and Benny, who had not previously met – Hedlund had joined the Hep Stars after the talent contest which Elverkets Spelmanslag and the Hep Stars had both entered – became friendly, and a few months later, when the Hep Stars and their keyboard player fell out and the keyboard player left the band, Benny was invited to replace him for one gig. As Elverkets Spelmanslag had virtually disbanded by this time, and Benny was working as a salesman of domestic appliances to make ends meet, although he hated the job, he was delighted to work with the Hep Stars, and soon afterwards, shortly before his 18th birthday, he joined the band permanently.

Despite their growing popularity, particularly after Benny joined the band, the Hep Stars had yet to make a hit record, and the label to which they were signed was starting to grow impatient that this new band was failing to deliver the goods. One of the problems was that none of the band members claimed to be songwriters, which meant that anything they recorded at that point was inevitably a cover version. In an attempt to rectify the situation, the group released three singles simultaneously in early 1965, all cover versions, but in two of the three cases, of somewhat obscure songs. One was Farmer John, which had been a US Top 20 hit in 1964 for the Premiers, a Californian group, although it is probably more likely that the Hep Stars heard it from an early LP by Merseybeat group, the Searchers. A second cover version was of a 1961 British hit by Mike Berry, Tribute to Buddy Holly, while the third was the rather more familiar Summertime Blues, a late 1950s classic by Eddie Cochran. However, none of these singles significantly changed the situation for the Hep Stars, and it wasn't until Svenne Hedlund heard a song on the radio, which turned out to be a cover version of the Vince Taylor rockabilly classic, Brand New Cadillac, but retitled simply Cadillac, that he felt he had possibly at last found a hit for the Hep Stars.

The record label was initially unenthusiastic, but after the group performed a highly uninhibited version of the song on television, jumping around the stage and climbing on loud speaker cabinets, they were suddenly stars with a substantial teenage following. This was the era of the British beat group, with the Beatles, the Rolling Stones, the Kinks, the Who and hundreds of others acts dominating the world's charts, and the Hep Stars became one of the biggest Swedish bands of the time – according to Carl Magnus Palm's book, Benny had wheels fitted to his organ so that he could move the instrument around the stage as he played it. The result of the television appearance was that Cadillac topped the Swedish singles chart, while Tribute to Buddy Holly reached the Top 10, and Farmer John also made Number 1. It was somewhat similar, although to a far lesser extent, to what happened for the Beatles in the USA, where in one week in March 1964, the group held all the top five positions as well as seven more positions in the Top 100.

The Hep Stars had arrived! However, a wild and raucous stage show did not necessarily result in huge record sales, and there is an interesting parallel between the mid-sixties popularity of the Hep Stars in Sweden, and the appeal of one of Britain's premier punk/rock acts in the late 1970s, the Clash. Coincidentally, the Clash also covered Brand New Cadillac on their London Calling album, but sales of their early recordings were largely restricted to enthusiastic fans who were perhaps more interested in the group's ethos and philosophy than in their records, while critics and those who were more interested in actually listening to the group's musical talents, were initially somewhat dismissive, as the last word that could be used to describe early Clash recordings was polished, which founder member Mick Jones later admitted. Eventually, the Clash did break through in the USA, although their only platinum-certified album, 1982's Combat Rock, was produced by Glyn Johns, who had made his name by producing non-punk acts like the Steve Miller Band, the Eagles, Joan Armatrading and Eric Clapton.

What the Hep Stars needed was original material, and the only member of the group who displayed any enthusiasm for writing an original song was Benny, who in 1965 came up with No Response, which he regards as his first significant composition, although he was more confident about the melody than the lyrics. Nevertheless, No Response reached the Top 3 of the Swedish singles chart, and the group's popularity continued to grow. Their first single of 1966, Sunny Girl, was another song written by Benny, and this was an even bigger success, topping the Swedish chart for several weeks, and the follow-up, Wedding, was written by Benny and Hep Stars' vocalist and frontman, Svenne Hedlund, who by all accounts was the teenage heart-throb of the band, and collaborated with Benny on the song's lyrics.

Wedding became another Swedish Number 1 single, and Benny had become a highly successful songwriter with three consecutive hits, including two chart-toppers. According to Carl Magnus Palm's book, the Hep Stars were responsible for ten per cent of record sales in Sweden in 1966, an extraordinary achievement. That year also brought the historic meeting between Benny Andersson and Björn Ulvaeus, who were at the time the main songwriters in their respective groups, and during a party attended by both bands, the two decided that it might be interesting to write a song together, which turned out to be Isn't it Easy to Say. Although this was far from the quality of most of the songs they later wrote, first for ABBA and later, collaborating with Tom Rice, for the Chess musical, it was the first Andersson/Ulvaeus collaboration, and thus of historical, if not necessarily of musical and aesthetic, significance. As well as writing together, there was also a sign of what was to follow when the Hep Stars recorded No Time, a song Björn had written which had been a hit for the Hootenanny Singers, while the latter group had recorded Benny's Sunny Girl on one of their albums

The bond between Benny and Björn grew stronger when the guitarist with the Hep Stars was stuck in Spain and unable to return to Sweden to play a couple of gigs, whereupon Björn was invited to deputise, which he did, with some success. However, Björn returned to the Hootenanny Singers, although his heart was seemingly no longer in the folk music they played. Meanwhile, the Hep Stars retained their popularity, even appearing on the highly rated British TV show, Dee Time, but clearly the business people who were theoretically looking after the financial and other aspects of the group's career, were failing in their duties – for example, the spot on Dee Time featured a song which was not available on record in Britain. Benny, meanwhile, had broken off his engagement to Christina Gronvall. He was always working with the group and simply had no time to see either Christina or his children, but he was now, to all intents and purposes, very available and excellent marriage material for ambitious young ladies, a situation which was magnified when the Hep Stars launched their own company, Hep House, which bore similarities to Apple, the company launched by the Beatles, and ironically experienced similar problems to those which afflicted Apple.

In early 1967, someone suggested that the group should star in a feature movie, once again, aping the Beatles. Unfortunately, the Hep Stars did not have a manager as devoted to them as Brian Epstein was to the Beatles (although Epstein has been judged to be far from error-free in his business dealings, and in fact had died before the launch of Apple, so was unable to protect or direct his charges) and were convinced that the movie should be made in Nairobi, Kenya. The resulting hours of footage have never been seen, although a number of directors have attempted, without success, to create a meaningful film from this embarrassment of riches. This was, of course, an extremely expensive undertaking for which the group footed the bill, yet saw no income whatsoever. If this disaster weren't serious enough, at the end of 1967, it became clear that not one member of the band had paid any income tax for some time, despite earning a relative fortune, probably because their so-called management had neglected to advise them that they would almost inevitably be found out. Also inevitably, Hep House went bankrupt and the group members had to shell out huge payments to clear their names and reputations.

In 1969, after Svenne Hedlund's black American girl-friend, Charlotte Walker, had joined the Hep Stars as vocalist – she had a 1962 US Top 40 hit, Pop Pop Pop-Pie, to her credit as a member of Philadelphia R&B act, the Sherrys – the Hep Stars fell apart, with Benny, Svenne and 'Lotta' leaving to work together, but that didn't last long, and Björn and Benny began working together more seriously. Also at the end of 1969, Benny and Anni-Frid became engaged, and began living together in Stockholm.

By then, Björn had also begun a relationship. After seeing on television a beautiful blonde girl with a wonderful voice named Agnetha Fältskog, he was smitten. Agnetha Ase Fältskog was born on 5 April 1950 in Jonkoping in the south of Sweden, and one of the other things which Björn liked about her was that she herself had written the song she had performed. Her father had been involved in local amateur dramatics, and encouraged his daughter to perform in front of audiences at local functions, but the major influence for the infant was playing a piano belonging to a neighbour, and when she was seven years old her parents bought her a piano of her own. She was also a huge fan of the work of Connie Francis, the Italian/American vocalist who is described in the chart 'bible', Billboard Top Pop Singles 1955 – 1996 as 'Pop music's #1 female vocalist from the late 1950s to the mid-1960s'. Constance Franconero

Anni-Frid and Agnetha perform live on television

accumulated 56 US hit singles between late 1957 and early 1969, including three Number Ones: Everybody's Somebody's Fool and My Heart Has a Mind of its Own (both 1960) and Don't Break the Heart that Loves You (1962) and seven million sellers. Her career was interrupted for four years from 1974 when she was raped, but, happily, she returned to singing in the late 1970s.

Agnetha became a top class pianist, and was part of an all-girl trio, but when she left school in 1965, she worked in an office, which allowed her to pursue her love of music at weekends, when she would sing with local orchestras. Eventually, in 1966, when the girl singer of a local orchestra left, Agnetha was invited to audition as her replacement, and soon proved to be a very quick learner, effortlessly performing R&B material by the likes of James Brown and Ray Charles, which were often requested at the American military bases where the band were a popular attraction.

She also continued with her songwriting, which she had started, amazingly, at the age of six, but which began seriously when she was 16. Her first major composition was a song whose title in English was I Was so in Love, which greatly impressed the leader of the orchestra, who soon included the song in his repertoire, but perhaps more importantly, contacted his wife's brother, who had been a Swedish rock star known as Little Gerhard, and who had graduated to becoming a talent scout for the CBS-Cupol record label. Little Gerhard immediately invited Agnetha to Stockholm to record the song formally, and when he heard the result, signed her to CBS-Cupol, for whom she recorded it. Because it is never easy to launch an unknown artist, it took some time for the general public in Sweden to become aware of the single, but when Agnetha performed it on television, which was her first appearance on the small screen, the single began to take off, and in early 1966 it reached the top of the Swedish chart. At this point, Agnetha was still working in an office by day and performing with the local orchestra in the evenings, as well as trying to promote her record releases by doing interviews with press and radio, and in early 1968 she collapsed with exhaustion, and was given the choice of either continuing with her singing career or giving it up and working in an office. She chose to continue singing, of course…

To some extent because she was a pretty blonde teenage girl, efforts were made to launch Agnetha's career in Germany, which was still divided by the Berlin Wall at the time. Other Swedish artists had been successful in West

Germany, so Agnetha was signed to Metronome Records, and that spring saw her recording in Berlin with producer Dieter Zimmerman, apparently a handsome 25 year old, and a mutual attraction arose between producer and artist. Agnetha was unable to remain in Berlin after finishing recording with Zimmerman as she was contracted to work with the orchestra back in Sweden, and on the same show as the orchestra were the Hootenanny Singers, which, of course, included Björn Ulvaeus, and that was where Björn and Agnetha first met face to face. Björn, by all accounts, was massively impressed by the beautiful young blonde, while Agnetha was also impressed by Björn, although she had other things on her mind at the time, notably Dieter Zimmerman, who had apparently agreed to promote Agnetha's compositions in Germany, while she, in return, would record songs he had written. To seal the arrangement, Dieter and Agnetha announced their engagement. Agnetha was 18 years old, and had moved to Stockholm to be closer to the centre of the Swedish music scene, but she discovered that the songs Zimmerman had written for her to record were not to her taste, nor were they successful in either Sweden or Germany. Added to this was the fact that the engaged couple were unable to agree on where they should live after getting married, Zimmerman favouring Germany and Agnetha Sweden, and eventually the pressures of rarely seeing each other caused the engagement to be called off.

Agnetha's career in Sweden continued to be successful as she returned to recording her own songs, and in 1969 she found herself on a television programme which featured a number of Swedish music stars, one of whom was Björn Ulvaeus.

By the end of the 1960s, Benny and Björn, both feeling that their respective groups were coming to the end of their useful lives, had formalised a songwriting and production partnership with their own company, Union Songs, in which their partner was Stig Anderson, who was anxious for them to write songs with lyrics in English rather than Swedish. According to Carl Magnus Palm's book, one of their first projects was to write songs which would be featured in a soft-porn movie, Inga II, and two of the songs they wrote for the movie, She's My Kind of Girl and Inga Theme, were the two sides of their first single released under the name Björn & Benny.

Meanwhile, with Dieter Zimmerman now history, Agnetha began a relationship with Björn, and they became engaged in October 1969, two months after Benny and Anni-Frid had done the same. Now the future members of ABBA were two engaged couples, although professionally, Agnetha and Anni-Frid were operating as soloists, while Benny and Björn were working together, making an album titled Lycka, although they were obviously also showing an interest in the careers of their fiancées. Agnetha had become very popular, to the point where two separate songs which she had written and recorded in 1969 were controversial. One was Gypsy Friend (Swedish title: Zigenarvän), for which she wrote the music but not the lyrics, which concerned a contemporary row about gypsies in Sweden (which was clearly not intentional, but perhaps made tabloid headlines – if the latter disease had affected Sweden all those years ago), while the other, If Tears Were Gold (Swedish title: On Tårar Vore Guld) was the subject of a threatened lawsuit for plagiarism by a Danish bandleader who claimed that part of a song he had written had been copied by Agnetha. It seems that the bandleader was trying too hard, for two reasons: firstly, he claimed to have written the song and performed it on a tour of Sweden in 1950, the year Agnetha was born, and although she was a child prodigy, it would be expecting too much for her to remember a tune so precisely before she was one year old (if indeed she had ever heard it, which she denied), and secondly, as he had never recorded the song, she would have been unable to hear it on record either. It is probably true to say that those who are very successful in music have always been subject to 'nuisance' lawsuits, the idea being to settle such claims out of court. As the much-quoted music business expression would have it, where there's a hit, there's also a writ...

By this time, Benny was producing Anni-Frid's recordings, although the impression seems to be that Anni-Frid's solo work before ABBA was of less interest to the Swedish general public than seeing her sparkling live performances. This changed somewhat when Benny produced a single for her which became only her second to reach the local chart, a Swedish version of Edison Lighthouse's Love Grows (Where My Rosemary Goes).

One of ABBA's trademarks is the group's extraordinarily perfect vocal harmonies, and this points back to one of the group's major influences, The Mamas and The Papas. The four members of that group were all hippies, half male and half female, they had all paid their dues on the New York folk circuit, and they went to The Virgin Islands for a holiday together during which they started harmonising and came up with one of the greatest sounds of the mid-1960s. Something similar happened to the four members of ABBA when the two couples shared their first holiday together in Cyprus. Benny and Björn took their guitars with them for campfire singalongs, and when Anni-Frid and Agnetha joined in, the harmonies were breathtaking, whereas separately, the male voices had frankly been OK, but not distinctive, while both Anni-Frid and Agnetha could be lead singer on tracks which suited their styles more. Anni-Frid preferred sophisticated and perhaps jazzy songs, while Agnetha felt that Connie Francis-styled ballads were her strong point. In fact, although ultimately Agnetha sang lead on more of ABBA's biggest hits, the voices of the girls were not easy to identify specifically, and it was sometimes only after seeing the video clip that one could be sure of who was singing lead.

Inevitably, this resulted in the quartet performing together, and the first time that this happened in public was in November 1970 when Björn and Benny were booked to appear at a Gothenburg restaurant on a night when neither Anni-Frid nor Agnetha was working. They devised a simple show and appeared all together, calling the quartet 'Festfolk', a Swedish phrase which can either mean 'party people' or 'engaged couples'. This first public performance by the quartet was hardly a success, as few punters seemed too interested, so the four returned to what they had been doing before, with Benny working on Anni-Frid's recordings and Björn on Agnetha's. Björn & Benny's Lycka album was apparently designed to show off their songwriting ability, and involved all four future members of ABBA on a track titled Hey Old Man (Swedish title: Hej Gamle Man), but Swedish record buyers were not particularly interested in the album, which was, after all, designed more to give exposure to songs written by Björn & Benny than to scale the heights of the chart. However, Hey Old Man became a substantial hit in Sweden, convincing the quartet that their potential line-up had real possibilities. Nevertheless, the constant proximity of living and working with the same person was sometimes hard to deal with, and would recur many times during the ABBA years.

Perhaps the single most important event of 1971 was when Björn and Agnetha were married on 6 July at a very old church in the village of Venum in the south of Sweden. However, the clergyman who was going to perform the ceremony misheard the couple's reply when he asked them about their professions; they replied that they were artists, but the preacher thought they had said they were Atheists, and indicated that he wasn't really prepared to marry two non-believers in a church. However, the confusion was cleared up, and the wedding took place. Although one reason for the choice of church had been that it was not a well-known place, which theoretically could be kept secret, word soon circulated and around 3,000 people came to see the two plight their troth. In the melee close to the church, one of the horses which was pulling the open coach in which the newly married couple were to reach the church stepped on Agnetha's foot, but her injury was not serious, and the ceremony went ahead. Anni-Frid was unable to attend, as she was on tour at the time, but Benny played an old Hep Stars hit, Wedding, on the church organ. During that summer, Björn, Agnetha and Benny were working together on a tour of Swedish 'folk parks', which were (and still are) outdoor venues where music is played during the summer months.

Only one cloud marred what was otherwise a day to remember. Bengt Bernhag, who, you may remember, was Stig Anderson's partner in Polar Music, suffered from colitis, and found it necessary to wear a colostomy bag, which made him very conscious of his disability to the point where he rarely left his home. On Björn and Agnetha's wedding day, Bernhag, who had been invited to the wedding, but felt so lacking in self-confidence that he decided not to go, was very depressed, and committed suicide by filling his car with exhaust fumes. It was a tragedy, but one which resulted in another major step forward in the formation of ABBA.

Without his partner, Stig Anderson had an important vacancy in the establishment of Polar Music, and the obvious person to whom he could offer the job of producer was, of course, Björn. A salary was mentioned, but Björn would not take the job unless Benny was also involved. When Stig said he couldn't afford to pay twice the salary, Björn said he would take half of what was offered, and Benny could take the other half. It almost goes without saying that Björn was certain that Benny must be his songwriting partner, and indeed their skills complement each other: Benny is a musical giant, but lyrics are not really his scene, whereas Björn's lyrics were visibly improving. Quite how Stig felt that Agnetha and Anni-Frid would be involved is hard to guess, and this was to some extent explained when Björn and Agnetha decided to record a duet celebrating their romance. Because Agnetha was signed to CBS-Cupol, that label claimed the rights to release the duet, but Stig argued that now Björn was not only signed to Polar Music, but worked for the label, that it should be released by Polar. The result was that the release of the track was delayed for some time.

However, early 1972 saw major success in the unlikely region of Japan. Björn & Benny's recording of She's My Kind of Girl, the song they had written for the soft-porn movie, Inga II, was released there, and topped the local chart, allegedly selling a quarter of a million copies. This level of success resulted in its writers being invited to submit an entry for a Japanese Song Festival to be held in Tokyo, where they were invited to perform the song, and unsurprisingly took their fiancées with them. The song they had written, Santa Rosa, was by their own admission below standard, and was initially titled I'd Give Anything to Be Back Home in…, with the place name inserted at the end of the line. The Japanese trip ultimately achieved very little.

However, about a week later, Björn and Benny wrote a much more suitable song titled Merry-Go-Round, and on the day they recorded it, with Agnetha and Anni-Frid taking part, they also conceived and recorded a new song, People Need Love, which has been compared with a similar song, Melting Pot, a 1969 UK Top 3 hit, by a band with a similar line-up, Blue Mink, part of whose appeal was the blend of male (Roger Cook) and female (Madeline Bell) voices. Björn has subsequently suggested that People Need Love was a blend of a Blue Mink hit (not necessarily Melting Pot) and Scottish group Middle Of The Road's massive (if slightly hysterical) 1971 five week UK chart-topper, Chirpy Chirpy Cheep Cheep, which was a hit in 20 countries and is believed to have sold over ten million copies, although in the USA a version by Mac & Katie Kissoon just made the Top 20 of the singles chart, while Lally Stott, the Liverpudlian composer of the song, also had a minor hit with his version in America.

When People Need Love was released as a single in Sweden in 1972, it became a big hit, even though the label on the record credited the artists as Björn, Benny, Agnetha and Anni-Frid, to which Stig Anderson had understandably objected strongly, on the basis that it was unwieldy, although Benny and Björn eventually insisted. Readers with strong attention spans may recall that this was the single released on Playboy Records in the USA, which came fairly close to the Top 100 singles chart, and was the first ABBA single, although the label on the Playboy single credited 'Björn & Benny (with

Svenska Flicka)'. Due to all the activity discussed above, including Björn and Agnetha's marriage, Bengt Bernhag's death, Agnetha's songwriting lawsuits, Benny's parting with Christina Gronvall, the 'Festfolk' fiasco, the break up of both the Hep Stars and the Hootenanny Singers, etc. People Need Love was not only the first Swedish hit single that any of the quartet had released for several years, but also the first time both Anni-Frid and Agnetha had figured on the Swedish radio chart, which for some reason was regarded as more important aesthetically, as opposed to the sales chart; Anni-Frid's appearance in the sales chart was also a first for her. Her time recording for the Swedish EMI label had not been a great success commercially, and Stig Anderson took the opportunity to sign her, keeping her under his Polar Music umbrella with Björn and Benny.

By the last quarter of 1972, the four future members of ABBA were recording material for what was intended to be their first formal album together, which would include both People Need Love and a follow-up single, He Is Your Brother, which topped the Swedish radio chart. This was a sufficient reason for Swedish broadcasting bosses to invite the songwriting team of Stig Anderson, Benny Andersson and Björn Ulvaeus to submit a song for the Swedish heat of the 1973 Eurovision Song Contest.

Historically, very few non-British acts which had been winners of the Eurovision Song Contest had managed to maintain a chart career in the UK after their Eurovision hit had ended its commercial life, although as has already been mentioned, Gigliola Cinquetti had managed a second hit (albeit another Eurovision-related song) ten years after her 1964 Eurovision victory. The history of the Eurovision Song Contest includes several possibly interesting items relating to either the songs entered for the contest or the artists who performed them. For example, in 1958 Britain didn't even enter the contest, which was won for Italy by Domenico Modugno with Nel Blu Dipinto Di Blu, which topped the US singles chart and made the Top 10 of the UK equivalent. This is a song which is more familiar under its UK title of Volare, and was a UK Top 3/US Top 20 hit for Dean Martin in 1958, the same year when it was a UK Top 30 hit for comedian Charlie Drake, and a US Top 100 hit for The McGuire Sisters, while Bobby Rydell's 1960 cover version made the US Top 5 and the UK Top 30. Finally (at the time of writing), Al Martino's 1975 revival was a US Top 40 hit. Which goes to prove that not everything produced by the Eurovision Song Contest is worthless, which has certainly been the perception in Britain from time to time.

A couple of examples from the 1960s: Greek vocalist Nana Mouskouri, whose UK chart career includes a Top 3 single and a string of hit albums during the period 1969-2001, represented Luxembourg in the 1963 contest (but didn't win that year), and in 1969 a then unknown Elton John & Bernie Taupin wrote a song for the UK Eurovision heat, which was rejected in favour of Lulu's highly intellectual Boom Bang-a-Bang, which came first equal with three other no doubt similarly intelligent songs (from France, Spain and Holland).

The 1970s brought some improvement. All Kinds of Everything by Irish girl-next-door Dana was the winner in 1970, beating Mary Hopkin, representing Britain with Knock Knock, Who's There? into second place, while a Spanish fellow named Julio Iglesias came fourth. Waterloo launched an international career for ABBA in 1974, and their song and performance was a massive improvement over a great many Eurovision winners, but the following year, 1975, brought a reversion to the somewhat dubious standard which had been prevalent before Waterloo. The Shadows came only second with Let Me Be the One, behind the Dutch entry, Teach In, with Ding-a-Dong, which made the UK Top 20, after which…? 1976 saw a British winner with Brotherhood Of Man's Save Your Kisses for Me, and it was noticed by more than a few that this combo of predominantly session vocalists seemed to be trying to copy ABBA, which was repeated in 1977 and 1978, respectively, with their UK chart-toppers, Angelo and Figaro.

The real point is that after ABBA had won Eurovision and topped the UK singles chart with Waterloo, the vast majority of the Great British public probably expected them to disappear, and certainly their next three singles gave little indication that ABBA would become massive international stars during the remainder of the 1970s. However, they did enjoy brief UK chart success with the Waterloo LP, which briefly reached the Top 30 of the UK album chart. While this was obviously designed to take advantage of the title track's Eurovision win and chart-topping achievement, the album was not a throwaway, apart from the fact that for many buyers, Waterloo was the only song they knew.

The Waterloo LP was not, of course, the first ABBA album to be released in Sweden, where the Ring Ring album had been released in 1973, although it was not easily available in the UK until 1992, after Polygram had purchased the rights to the Polar Music catalogue. A few tracks which appear on the Ring Ring album have already been mentioned, like the title track, and Rock'n'Roll Band, its B-side when it was first released as a UK single in 1973, People Need Love, He Is Your Brother, etc., as well as both sides of the single released in Sweden after He Is Your Brother, but before Ring Ring, Love Isn't Easy (But it Sure Is Hard Enough) and I Am Just a Girl. Of the other tracks, Disillusion was written by Agnetha (tune) and Björn (lyrics), and is the only song released by ABBA which Agnetha had a hand in writing, while I Saw it in the Mirror, on which Björn and Benny are lead vocalists, is of minimal interest. Nina Pretty Ballerina was released as a single in France, and the strangely-titled Me and Bobby and Bobby's Brother bears the mark of a relatively inexperienced lyricist – Björn swiftly improved on this – and She's My Kind of Girl had been a hit in Japan and was probably the best song written for the Inga II soundtrack. Like many debut albums, Ring Ring was far from perfect, but provides an interesting picture of ABBA a year before they became famous. It was a sizeable hit in Sweden, but, with the benefit of hindsight, would probably have been ignored if it had been released in the UK or the USA when ABBA were unknown.

Six weeks after the release of the Waterloo single, it was followed by the album of the same title, which includes three songs crediting Stig Anderson as songwriter along with Björn and Benny, who were solely responsible for the other nine songs. Waterloo was one of the three, while the others were Honey Honey and Hasta Mañana, the latter a Spanish phrase meaning 'see you tomorrow', which was a strong contender as ABBA's entry for the Swedish Eurovision heat before Stig decided on Waterloo, but was finally rejected because only Agnetha was lead vocalist on the song. Waterloo equally featured both Anni-Frid and Agnetha, which was what, it was felt, would be required to win Eurovision (or at least the Swedish heat). Honey Honey had been slated as the follow-up single to Waterloo in some countries, but because Epic in Britain still believed that Ring Ring was a potential hit, Honey Honey was not released as an ABBA single in Britain. However, the song did become a Top 10 hit in the hands of Sweet Dreams, a boy and girl duo who seemingly never had another hit, although in 1983 an identically-named British vocal group with both male and female members represented the UK in that year's Eurovision Song Contest, but were far from winning with their song I'm Never Giving Up - which they probably did after their Eurovision failure, although when it was released as a UK single, it almost made the Top 20.

Back to the Waterloo album – Carl Magnus Palm's book correctly identifies the fact that the best tracks are those on which the girls are featured, the three which Stig was involved in writing as well as Dance (While the Music Still Goes On) and Gonna Sing You My Love Song. The titles of songs like Sitting in the Palm tree King Kong Song and What about Livingstone? suggest novelty items as opposed to solid and worthy compositions, but bearing in mind that no one could possibly know what the future had in store for the quartet, these songs, while clearly not candidates for release as singles, were not obvious filler material.

Arguably the greatest advantage to ABBA earned by the Waterloo single and album was that they were a launch pad for the quartet in the USA, where the group were signed to Atlantic Records, a most unlikely home for a Swedish pop group who had just won Eurovision. Atlantic shares with Motown the title of the pioneering soul labels of the rock era, although Atlantic is about ten years older, having started activity in 1947. The major names which are umbilically attached to Atlantic include Ray Charles, the Drifters, the Coasters, LaVern Baker, Chuck Willis, Otis Redding, Aretha Franklin, Wilson Pickett, Percy Sledge, Solomon Burke, Buffalo Springfield, Led Zeppelin, Yes, Crosby, Stills, Nash & Young and others, and while in retrospect it is clear that ABBA would ultimately qualify for that level of fame, in 1974 it seemed far less certain. Apparently, various high flyers in the European record industry had recommended to Atlantic that ABBA were well worth checking out, especially after CBS, to whose Epic subsidiary ABBA were signed for the UK, displayed little interest in signing them for the US. Although they had made minor waves with People Need Love a couple of years earlier, the quartet were to all intents and purposes unknown in the biggest record market in the world, and a lot of work would be necessary to alter that situation. The key to success in the USA is for any act to appear there, but, for ABBA, this would have been impossible for several reasons, the main one being that Agnetha did not want to leave her daughter, Linda, who was less than 18 months old at the time, for a promotional tour of such a vast country, which would probably have taken a minimum of two months.

However, the Waterloo single did remarkably well, making the Top 10 of the Billboard US singles chart, where it was listed for four months, and briefly making the Top 150 of the equivalent album chart during a two month stay. This was a very good start, and, knowing that for the group to have been there in person would probably have produced a better result led to the decision by ABBA to make a film clip of themselves performing Waterloo, which could then be screened in territories where the band were unable to schedule a visit. This would have huge implications for their future success, although no one realised it at the time.

The next step was choosing a single to follow Waterloo, and in the two important territories where ABBA had broken through, different follow-up singles were chosen. In Britain, it was decided that Ring Ring should have another chance, and this time it performed slightly better, nearly reaching the Top 30, while in the US, Honey Honey, which was the chosen track, spent ten weeks in the chart, peaking inside the Top 30. However, this was ABBA's farewell to the US chart for many months, despite a brief (three day) promotional trip to America, where they appeared on the highly-rated Mike

A glimpse of the band's staging from a live show on tour

Douglas Show, and even in the UK things did not seem to be progressing as planned. Björn and Benny had recorded several new tracks with their fiancées for a new album, and it was decided that So Long, a song in similar vein to Waterloo, should be the new single, while its flipside, I've Been Waiting for You, was a ballad whose lyrics had involved Stig Anderson, who presumably thought this was a stronger track, and one on which he could use his lyrical expertise. The single was released in Britain at the end of November 1974, but perhaps the timing was wrong – less than a month before Christmas – and perhaps the wrong track had been chosen as the one to be promoted. Whatever it was, this became the only UK single released by ABBA in the 1970s which completely failed to reach the UK chart. The curse of Eurovision seemed to have struck again!

The start of 1975 must have been a difficult time for ABBA and everyone connected with them. After making some reasonable progress after their Eurovision win, the hits had ended on both sides of the Atlantic, although the group had actually performed a handful of live concerts in both Scandinavia and the GAS countries (Germany, Switzerland and Austria) in late 1974 and early 1975. It had been intended that the tour should have been much more extensive and also cover Britain, France, Holland, Spain, Greece and even some of the countries which, at the time, were part of Yugoslavia. This was the tour during which Agnetha was somewhat embarrassed when a journalist wrote that she had the sexiest bottom in popular music, although many agreed with the sentiment.

Still with the problem of returning to the UK chart after the debacle of So Long, the next track released as a single in Britain was probably designed to demonstrate that ABBA were not limited in the musical styles which seemed available to them. In April, 1975, the nostalgic-sounding I Do, I Do, I Do, I Do, I Do, another track from the forthcoming new album, appeared, and was promoted to British radio with all the muscle and expense that the promotion department of Epic Records could muster. Three male staff hired wedding outfits, and while one dressed as a bridegroom, another was a pretend Best Man, and the third a rather unconvincing bride. They were driven in a Rolls Royce to present the single to the all-important BBC Radio One producers and disc jockeys, and other media, which would hopefully divert attention away from the very dated sound of the track. Although the single, which brings to mind female vocal acts of the pre-rock era such as the Andrews Sisters, was a hit, and thus was more successful than So Long, Melody Maker were not merely dismissive when the newspaper's reviewer wrote 'This single is so bad, it hurts'. Even so, the single, which briefly reached the UK Top 40, at least boasted a flip side, Rock Me, which sounded, as its title suggested, like rock music, and featured a lead vocal by Björn. Rock Me was in extreme contrast to the antique sound of the rather repetitive I Do, I Do, I Do, I Do, I Do, which was one of six tracks on the ABBA album for which Stig Anderson was credited as composer with Björn and Benny.

In May 1975, what had been heard of the new ABBA album did not augur well for its success: two flop singles, whose flip sides were preferable in both cases. What few can have known, other than those privileged to hear the complete album prior to its release in early June, was that it included two extremely strong tracks which sounded like certain hits, and which would transform ABBA from Eurovision rejects to international stars. The breakthrough single, which totally reversed the downward trend for ABBA, was SOS. According to Billboard, this is the only US hit where both the song title and the name of the act/artist are palindromes, which read the same from left to right and from right to left. In the US, SOS became ABBA's third hit single in August 1975, peaking well inside the Top 20 and stayed in the chart until Xmas. SOS was a certain hit in the UK, but it was not released until three months after the ABBA album, probably to ensure that Radio One, the predominant and only national station for pop and rock fans at the time, liked the song. The album itself was cause for concern, taking six months to reach the UK chart, and peaking only inside the Top 20 during a ten week residency, which it did early in 1976, by which time SOS had entered the singles chart in September, peaking inside the Top 10 and staying in the chart twice as long as either Ring Ring or I Do, etc. This drew attention to the album, which was multiplied when the next single, released in November, 1975, was Mamma Mia, later, of course, the title of the incredibly successful stage musical which features ABBA's music.

The obstacles which this ABBA single overcame to reach the Number 1 position seem extraordinary in retrospect. The major problem was what may be regarded as one of the most extraordinary Number 1 singles of the rock era, Bohemian Rhapsody by Queen, which remained at the top for nine weeks from late November 1975 until the end of January 1976. But Mamma Mia (like SOS, with a songwriting credit for Stig Anderson as well as Björn & Benny) had enough staying power to reach Number 1 on the last day of January. The flip sides of both the SOS and Mamma Mia singles were written by Benny & Björn and were also included on the album. In chronological order, Man in the Middle is the favourite ABBA track of very few, while Benny's impressive instrumental, Intermezzo No.1 displays his keyboard mastery in both popular and classical styles.

In the US, where ABBA spent two weeks on a promotional trip in November 1975, it was rather different. Following SOS, the first 1976 single was I Do, etc., which actually made the Top 20, which was followed three months later, in May 1976, by Mamma Mia, which surprisingly was a comparative disappointment, peaking outside the US Top 30. One reason might just be that the quality of the video clip of the song which is included here, from a 1976 edition of the highly-rated Midnight Special TV series, is uninspired, while the album's US chart performance was uninspiring – three weeks in the chart peaking well outside the Top 150 - although the album has the fairly rare distinction that each of its 11 tracks was released on one side or other of a single on one or both sides of the Atlantic; the reggae-ish Tropical Loveland was the US flipside of the Mamma Mia single, while Bang-a-Boomerang was the US flipside of I Do, I Do, I Do, I Do, I Do.

By the start of 1976, ABBA were in a good position in Britain, with two big hit singles after a year when everything seemed to be going wrong in the wake of their Eurovision triumph, and their upward progress continued, initially with a new single, Fernando, which was released in early March, but major success was also brewing in Australia, which would become the first territory outside Europe where ABBA became superstars.

By this time, they had started making visual clips to accompany each song, directed by Lasse Hallstrom, who had worked with great success for the Swedish national TV company, and was expert at producing excellent footage without spending a fortune. Hallstrom's first work for ABBA had been clips of Waterloo and Ring Ring, and he was then asked to do similar work for I Do, I Do, I Do, I Do, I Do, SOS, Mamma Mia and Bang-a-Boomerang, and these clips were sent to faraway countries like Australia and New Zealand, where a tour might be unlikely but plenty of records could be sold. In fact, ABBA

The band's publicity shot for the 1970s album Arrival

would not only tour in Australia, but would dominate the local chart to an unbelievable extent, nearly comparable with the week in April 1964 when the Beatles occupied the Top five positions in the US singles chart.

In April 1976, twelve years to the month after the Beatles conquered the USA, ABBA conquered Australia. Fernando was at Number 1, Ring Ring at Number 4, Rock Me at Number 5, Mamma Mia at Number 20, and SOS at Number 22, while all three ABBA albums were in the Top 20 of the Australian album chart. The story goes that a man who worked at a blood bank in Sydney named David Abba had to change his number to stop people ringing him and singing 'Can you hear the drums, Fernando?' The likelihood of this story being true is diminished when we learn that Mr Abba claimed never to have heard of the group who shared his surname... In fact, ABBA's massive Australian success was due to a couple of those Lasse Hallstrom film clips, which were screened on television and captivated the nation.

Before that, a new ABBA album had been released in the UK, with the slightly dubious title of Greatest Hits. This title was much more accurate in Sweden, as it not only included the international hits like Waterloo, Fernando and Mamma Mia, but also such early successes as He Is Your Brother and People Need Love. The fold-out sleeve showed the four group members sitting on a bench in a park, and while Anni-Frid and Benny are in a passionate embrace, Agnetha is looking ignored while Björn reads a newspaper. The image thus portrayed was unexpected, to say the least, but perhaps the group (and the girls in particular) wanted to prove that they were more than human muppets dressed up as glam rockers. The LP was a significant success in Britain, where it became the year's best selling album, and was the first of eight consecutive chart-topping albums for ABBA, retaining the top spot for nine weeks during May, June and July 1976, and returning to Number 1 for two weeks in October.

By contrast, in the US, the album was not released until September, but thereafter spent over a year in the US chart, becoming the group's first Top 50 album and being certified platinum. After the comparative failure in the US of the Mamma Mia single, which peaked outside the Top 30, Fernando was a definite improvement, becoming ABBA's fourth Top 20 single out of their total of six hits, but perhaps its inclusion on the Greatest Hits album resulted in sales being spread between the album and the single, and both suffered.

In March 1976 ABBA made their first trip to Australia, which they had not intended to do at that time, but demand from the general public there was so massive that a short visit became necessary, particularly as the main activity was filming a TV special, which was screened on a Saturday night and attracted more than 50 per cent of the Australian viewing audience, apparently a greater percentage than had watched the 1969 moon landing, which had attracted the previous biggest-ever Australian TV audience. Titled The Best of ABBA, the special, which by all accounts was of a reasonable, if not extraordinary, standard owed some of its appeal to the fact that it had been made in Australia for Australians, something which rarely, if ever, happened. An album, also titled The Best of ABBA, topped the local chart for four months and sold over 1.1 million units, which was apparently more than any other album had ever sold in Australia up to that point, and may still remain the biggest-ever selling album in Australia, while the Fernando single established a new Australian record by remaining at Number 1 for 14 weeks.

The 19th of June 1976 was a very special day in Sweden. King Carl Gustaf was to marry a young lady with whom he had fallen in love, Silvia Sommerlath, and the day before the Royal wedding, a gala was held in the future Queen's honour featuring all manner of famous Swedish performers, although ABBA were the sole representatives of pop music. The song they performed before the Royal couple was a new composition they had only just completed, and was titled Dancing Queen. It was inevitable that someone would suggest the song had been specially written for the occasion, but, by all accounts, this was completely inaccurate as the song had existed under the working title of Boogaloo since late 1975, according to Carl Magnus Palm's book. What an amazing promotional opportunity, to play Dancing Queen to genuine royalty!

The Dancing Queen single which, with its flipside, That's Me, were the first tracks to be heard from the forthcoming Arrival album, was an instant smash hit in Britain when it appeared in the first week of August, a date when, usually, few guaranteed hit singles are released. Within two weeks, it was Number 1, where it remained for six weeks. This was ABBA's biggest single hit, although it is rarely regarded by critics as the quartet's finest moment. Perhaps the problem was that the summer of 1976 brought several novelty hits to Number 1, including No Charge by J J Barrie, Combine Harvester by

The Wurzels and Excerpts from The Roussos Phenomenon by a Greek bloke in a tent. After all that, Don't Go Breaking My Heart by Sir Elton and Kiki Dee hogged Number 1 for six weeks before Dancing Queen passed it for its own six week spell. A simultaneous announcement that 1977 would see a world tour, which would include a London show, brought excitement to fever pitch. Now with four Number 1 singles and a chart-topping album to their credit, this would be the test. In the USA, Dancing Queen was released two weeks before Christmas 1976, and steadily climbed the singles chart for about three months until it finally reached Number 1 and sold a million copies to become ABBA's greatest moment in their struggle to conquer the biggest market in the world. With the benefit of hindsight, it becomes clear that to genuinely make it in the States, the only way is to tour the country again and again. ABBA simply weren't prepared to do that, for a variety of reasons.

One interesting side issue produced by Dancing Queen was the song's adoption by homosexuals and lesbians as a theme song which helped to identify them to others of a similar non-heterosexual inclination, and this movement grew in strength and remains prevalent today, although the opening bars of the song are guaranteed to fill dance floors in almost every circumstance.

November 1976 brought the release of the Arrival album, which was following the UK chart-topping success of Greatest Hits, and quite reasonably included both the Number 1 single, Dancing Queen, and a brand new single, Money, Money, Money, with lead vocal from Anni-Frid. This was an appropriate choice, since the song sounded as if it might have been from a theatrical production, and suited Anni-Frid's thespian talents.

The album was certain to attract attention, although it didn't reach the Number 1 slot until the third week in January, being outsold first by the TV-advertised 20 Golden Greats by Glen Campbell, and then by A Day at the Races by Queen. Even after such a marketing effort, Arrival was only able to hold the top spot for a single week, as more TV-advertised collections were released. The first, Red River Valley, a four week Number 1 by veteran American country star Slim Whitman, who yodeled his way into the hearts of, presumably, the elderly, was somewhat of a surprise, although it was much more predictable that national treasures (in the nicest possible way) the Shadows would enjoy huge success with 20 Golden Greats, which outsold everything else for six weeks, which included the entire month of March. The start of April brought another genuine superstar into contention, Frank Sinatra, and Portrait of Sinatra, Number 1 for a fortnight, meant that it was nearly three months between Arrival arriving at the top and regaining its position.

However, the Arrival album was by no means wall-to-wall hit singles and their B-sides Sure, Dancing Queen, Money, Money, Money and Knowing Me, Knowing You were all big hits, but there was plenty of other worthwhile stuff, such as the rocking Why Did it Have to Be Me, sung by Björn in the style of New Orleans pianists/vocalists such as Antoine 'Fats' Domino or Smiley Lewis. In fact, after the melody line for this song had been established, Björn and Benny favoured the R&B style which became Why Did it Have to Be, whereas Stig Anderson preferred using the melody line in a gentler style, which was eventually released, with different lyrics, of course, as the flipside of the Knowing Me, knowing You single, under the title of Happy Hawaii.

While songs like When I Kissed the Teacher, featuring Agnetha as lead vocalist, and her impassioned vocal on My Love, My Life, were what was expected of ABBA, Why Did it Have to Be Me revisited the style of Rock Me, which had been a big hit single in Australia, and the unfortunately-titled Dum Dum Diddle seemed like a reversion to Eurovision-style thinking, but the title track, an instrumental, was certainly unexpected. Arrival was another track for which Benny was the main inspiration. He had always been fascinated by an aspect of Swedish musical heritage involving local folk music which featured fiddle players, although this Celtic-sounding track also involved Benny playing several types of keyboard, including a mellotron and a mini-moog. Several members of a string section who were in the studio chiefly to work on My Love, My Life were also used on Arrival, a tune which was later covered by Mike Oldfield, the famous creator of the chart-topping Tubular Bells and Hergest Ridge albums. In fact, this track was apparently not expected to be included on the album originally, until the sleeve concept of the quartet pictured in a helicopter was decided upon, at which point the Arrival title was given to the track, which also featured wordless female vocals for added colour.

The release of Arrival in Britain had been planned as a headline-grabbing press conference to be held aboard the historic Mayflower, a ship that was

The girls photographed before a concert

anchored on the River Thames, and, to echo the album's sleeve photograph, the group would arrive at the ship on a helicopter. It all sounded like a great idea, but as it was November, thick fog prevented the helicopter from taking off, and the band had to get to the Mayflower by limousine, which meant they arrived an hour late. The album's release launched a period of world travel for ABBA. One of the most interesting aspects of their success had been that they had become megastars in such unlikely countries as Poland, at the time still ruled by Russian overlords, where the government had decreed that only a certain amount of Polish currency could be spent on buying US dollars. 'Greenbacks' were an infinitely more valuable currency and acceptable for importing records from the West, and in 1976 that entire budget was spent on over three quarters of a million copies of the Arrival album. ABBA had thousands of fans in Poland, which was the result of the address of the Swedish ABBA fan club being printed in a magazine and generating many thousands of letters from Poland. With devotion like this from Polish fans, Abba had felt obliged to visit the country and had made a TV special there. Another promotional trip was to the USA, where the quartet were guests on the Dinah Shore show. Ms Shore, a highly respected vocalist whose fame had started in the 1940s, had obviously read as much about her guests as she could find from research, and told Anni-Frid and Benny that she found it surprising that they had been engaged for so long without actually taking the final step of getting married, and offered them the chance to marry that very day on television. Thanks, but no thanks, was the polite answer.

With three successive UK chart-topping singles to their credit in the previous year, much was expected of the next ABBA single. Could they make it four Number Ones in a row? Perhaps the choice of Money, Money, Money was a little too sophisticated and perhaps also too much in the vein of 1930s German cabaret, when chanteuses like Marlene Dietrich became icons of the period between the First and Second World Wars, and decadence was a popular trend, as recognised in the hugely successful 1972 feature movie, Cabaret; which starred Judy Garland's daughter, Liza Minnelli, whose great performance won her a Best Actress Oscar award. Anni-Frid accepted with both hands the opportunity to sing this rather adult song, a considerable contrast to the usual ABBA output. From a 1978 Japanese TV Special, three songs are included: the almost inevitable SOS, a scintillating clip of Anni-Frid doing her best Dietrich impersonation and what must be one of the earliest filmed versions of the song that seems to have become accepted as ABBA's signature tune, Thank You for the Music.

Money, Money, Money also gave ABBA the chance to make an interesting film clip, but the single was released only a week after the Arrival album, which also included the song. It is mysterious that marketing managers should think that punters will buy a single which they already own as an album track, and while Crazy World, the flip-side of the single, is not on the album, the song hardly qualifies as one which every ABBA fan would be pleased to own. Sung by Björn, the song tells the story of how a boy sees another male who he doesn't recognise going into the house of his girlfriend. After spending some time being depressed because he thinks his girlfriend is being unfaithful, he eventually gains enough courage to ask her who the stranger is, and is relieved to discover that the stranger is, in fact, his girlfriend's brother. This Mills & Boon-esque plot cannot be termed one of ABBA's finest moments, although by contrast, Money, Money, Money is an impressive piece of work. It didn't become the fourth consecutive UK Number 1 for ABBA, but did make the Top 3, becoming ABBA's fifth single to reach those heights in three years.

On the other side of the Atlantic, things were, as usual, slightly different. Atlantic Records decided that instead of following the UK's release pattern, they preferred to let the Arrival album be the next ABBA product, and that was what happened. The album appeared in January 1977 and spent nearly a year in the Billboard chart, just peaking inside the Top 20, and receiving a promotional boost when Knowing Me, Knowing You was released as a single in May 1977 and became the sixth ABBA single to make the Top 20 of the US singles chart. In October that year, after Knowing Me, Knowing You had finally disappeared from the chart, Money, Money, Money was released as a US single, although it failed to reach the Top 50, probably because many ABBA fans in the US had already purchased the Arrival album on which Money, Money, Money also appeared.

By then, the group had just about recovered from their first world tour, which had begun at the end of January. This had included the first ever ABBA shows in Britain and Australia, after concerts in Scandinavia and other parts of Europe. Due to the massive expense of staging this tour, ABBA knew before they started, unlike many acts, that there was very little chance of making any profit because around 40 people were needed to erect, dismantle and move around the equipment, which included a 20,000 watt stereo PA system and 30 tons of lighting equipment. In addition, a backing group of a dozen musicians and singers were selected for this highly desirable task, and the cost for each day the show was on the road was apparently £9,000, which seems a trifle by twenty-first century standards, but at the time, almost 30 years ago, was regarded as monstrously expensive. The backing singers and musicians were as follows: on backing vocals were Lena Andersson (for whom, readers may recall, Benny & Björn had written a song which was placed third in the 1972 Swedish Eurovision heat), Lena-Maria Gardenas-Lawton and Maritza Horn, while horn players were Ulf Andersson and Lars Karlsson, with keyboard players Anders Eljas and Wojciech Ernest. There were two guitarists, Lasse Wellander and Finn Sjoberg, a rhythm section of Rutger Gunnarsson on bass and Ola Brunkert on drums, plus Malando Gassama, a black percussionist from Gambia on the west coast of Africa.

The British dates were two shows at London's Royal Albert Hall on St Valentine's Day, 14 February 1977, as well as shows in Birmingham, Manchester and Glasgow. The London show was ten days after the release of the new ABBA single, Knowing Me, Knowing You, the third single to be extracted from the Arrival album, following Dancing Queen and Money, Money, Money; ABBA fans should note that when the nine CDs of ABBA Remasters were released in 1997, Fernando was added as a bonus track, as the only previous album on which it had appeared was Greatest Hits, which was not part of the ABBA Remasters series. Knowing Me, Knowing You, despite the benefit of the group's first live appearances in Britain, took until the first week in April before it became ABBA's fifth UK Number 1 single, having to wait behind two other chart-toppers, Leo Sayer's When I Need You and Manhattan Transfer's Chanson d'Amour, which both spent three weeks at Number 1 before allowing ABBA to take its predictable place, where it remained for five weeks. The flip side of the single was Happy Hawaii, which, as mentioned previously, used the same tune as Why Did it Have to Be Me.

There were an incredible three and a half million applications for the 12,000 seats available over the two shows at the Royal Albert Hall, some indication of how the British had taken ABBA to their hearts. The shows began with the sound effect of a helicopter – a reminder of the sleeve image on the Arrival album – before the four members of ABBA onstage were picked out by spotlights. The show, which lasted for around 100 minutes, began with a specially written introductory song, I Am An A, designed to introduce each member of the group to those who had been on Mars since 1974, and included all the biggest hits plus most of the tracks from Arrival, the group's latest album, as well as some new material, the most impressive part of which was music and scenes from their incomplete (and seemingly never completed) projected 'mini-musical', The Girl with the Golden Hair. This provided an element of theatre as a British actor, for some reason dressed like a refugee from a Hammer horror movie, attempted to provide continuity of a sort. It is interesting to learn from Carl Magnus Palm's Bright Lights, Dark Shadows (almost certainly the most complete biography of ABBA ever written, and unreservedly recommended as a masterpiece) that the chorus of I Am An A, a song which was never released on record by the group, was used again to great effect in a much better known song titled I Know Him So Well, of which more later.

However, at least one song from The Girl with the Golden Hair must be well known to anyone with the slightest interest in ABBA. The song even includes the words 'The Girl with the Golden Hair', and is, of course, Thank You for the Music, which many regard as ABBA's signature tune, although when it was released as a single in 1983 it charted in Britain outside the Top 30. Three other songs from the mini-musical were performed, the best known of which was I Wonder (Departure), a live version of which became the flip side of the next ABBA single, while I'm a Marionette would be included on the next ABBA album, although Get on the Carousel, appears not to have been released on record by ABBA. My most abiding memory of this part of the show was when Agnetha and Anni-Frid, both wearing identically styled blonde wigs, were virtually indistinguishable, and frankly, had it not been for Thank You for the Music, the mini-musical would have been fairly forgettable, despite the efforts of the actor trying to provide links in a story line about a girl (with golden hair, of course) leaving her small hometown to seek fame and finding when she achieved fame that there are always drawbacks. British media were divided in their opinions of the live ABBA experience. One critic called the show 'the greatest thing since the Beatles', while another wrote that it was 'crass, glib and contrived', although Benny and Björn must have been delighted when Bart Mills (an American) wrote in The Daily Mail: 'Their singles have storylines and points of view which are as true an expression of today's well-fed Europe as Chuck Berry's songs were of 1950s America', while Richard Williams, arguably the doyen of early 1970s rock writing, praised the group's musical arrangements, saying they were inspired by the work of Brian Wilson and Phil Spector. To be mentioned in the same sentence as Berry, Wilson or Spector, must have been a massive compliment to Benny and Björn, while ABBA were apparently the first Swedish act to headline at the historic venue built by Queen Victoria in memory of her late husband, Prince Albert, who had suggested that there should be an arts complex in Kensington, opposite Hyde Park. Unfortunately, the prince sadly died before the plan came to fruition, although the Royal Albert Hall remains one of the most famous venues in the world.

Because it had already been decided that ABBA would not tour in 1978, one good reason being that by then Björn and Agnetha would have become parents for a second time, the idea of a film in which the group would star was mooted around this time. After initially planning a documentary, it was decided that a light comedy might be more appropriate, and the obvious backdrop would be the world tour. Thus when the group reached Australia, where they were already superstars, at the beginning of March 1977 they took with them Lasse Hallstrom, the man who had directed their video clips. The tour started controversially when an Australian magazine suggested that the four people who looked like ABBA were actually actors miming to their records, which, of course, was totally untrue, although ironically the world famous ABBA tribute band, Björn Again, were (and are) actors, although they actually play instruments and perform the songs extremely convincingly, and certainly do not mime to ABBA's records.

Despite upsetting rumours of subterfuge, the Australian tour was always going to be a triumph, and the 11 shows ABBA performed were watched by nearly 150,000 people, which was an incredible one per cent of the entire population of the country. Around 1,500 fans were at the airport in Sydney hoping to catch a glimpse of the group, but the rigours of such a lengthy flight – halfway round the world – meant that none of the band felt much like talking to anyone.

Having made the decision to make a movie centred around the Australian tour, a film crew was following the group everywhere. The 'plot' of the film was quite simple: the idea was that a disc jockey named Ashley (played by Australian actor Robert Hughes) had been given the task of conducting a lengthy interview with the members of ABBA during their time in Oz, but was constantly handicapped due to their extraordinarily busy schedule, and his journey across Australia was interspersed with live footage of the group's performances as they moved from venue to hotel to venue. In fact, when the ABBA – LIVE album was released in 1992, it included versions of Fernando and Money, Money, Money which were captured during the Australian tour.

The first two shows took place in Sydney. The first night's outdoor performance saw an audience of 20,000, who had waited in torrential rain for many hours, resulting in the venue becoming a mud bath, and the stage being covered in water, which made performing that much more difficult as it was dangerously slippery. Fortunately, the only casualty was Anni-Frid, who fell over at one point, although her injuries were comparatively slight. In addition, the rain made the use of electrified instruments, like Benny's keyboards, a major hazard; the rain had also penetrated the amplification equipment, making it difficult to produce the very clear sound which was required for an audience of that size. Even the members of ABBA were amazed at the enthusiasm with which their fans were prepared to wait in appalling conditions for the chance to see them perform, and, despite the potentially dangerous conditions, the group knew that it would have been unthinkable for the concert to be either cancelled or rescheduled. The second night at the same venue saw the weather considerably improved, although obviously conditions underfoot were hardly ideal. The next show was in Melbourne, where many thousands of fans lined the route from the airport and gathered to see the band at the Town Hall, and over 30,000 assembled in and around the concert venue, one of them being Australian Prime Minister, Malcolm Fraser, who clearly thought it would be good for his image to meet ABBA. However, his national unpopularity was so great at the time that his appearance was met with sustained booing. Adelaide was next, where the hysteria continued, with an audience of over 20,000 and half as many again listening from outside the football stadium where the group performed.

The last part of the Australian tour comprised five indoor shows in Perth,

Western Australia, each with 8,000 fans in the audience. The concert sound for these shows was much more manageable, and much of the film footage was shot at these shows, although there were complaints from audience members about onstage cameramen making the action hard to watch. But just to underline what a memorable, if exhausting, Antipodean visit it had been, the first Perth concert was interrupted by a bomb scare which sent both audience and performers out of the hall until a thorough search had been undertaken.

While from some aspects, the Australian tour had been a massive success, its stars were undoubtedly delighted when it was all over, and they could return to some kind of normality, which they had all increasingly wanted, especially Agnetha, who had greatly missed her daughter, Linda. Some group members were adamant that they would never undertake such a tour again, although two years later, they relented. At least the 1977 tour had brought the movie, which would enable them to have a necessary break from concerts, which was exactly the reason why Elvis Presley made several dozen movies in the 1960s – it enabled his fans all over the world to watch their idol without him having to travel to many countries, as the movies would carry his image and his songs around the world. The Beatles obviously did the same for similar reasons, and it is interesting that ABBA should also have adopted that approach, although, of course, ABBA only made one film, possibly because they realised that when ABBA – The Movie was completed and released, it was in all honesty not much of a showcase for their talents, other than proving that they could perform live just as well as making great records. Benny and Björn were probably especially unhappy with the results of their dalliance with the silver screen; Benny, in particular, had done it all before with the Hep Stars, and reportedly wasn't at all happy that ABBA were going down a similar route and might make similar mistakes.

In all honesty, Benny was quite correct to be concerned because ABBA – The Movie, although it features some footage of the group performing, is about as plotless as the vast majority of early exploitation rock movies. A complete concert movie would have been far more meaningful, as neither Agnetha nor Anni-Frid felt confident enough about their command of English to speak at any length when they were being filmed, which meant that the impression was given – quite incorrectly – that the group was dominated totally by Björn and Benny. ABBA visited Britain for the launch of the film in February 1978 and other pop/rock celebrities who attended the premiere included Pete Townshend, John Entwistle and Keith Moon, all members of the Who, as well as actress Connie Booth, erstwhile wife of John Cleese, and one of his co-stars in the massively successful Fawlty Towers TV series. During their four day stay, ABBA were also presented with the Carl Allen Songwriting Award by HRH Princess Margaret, the sister of English monarch Queen Elizabeth II.

One way in which the film was probably helpful was that in January 1978 ABBA released a new album which was titled and marketed to be a companion to the movie, and was titled ABBA – The Album. In the autumn of 1977, the first signs of what the album might contain were heard when a new single, The Name of the Game, was released, with a live recording of I Wonder (Departure) from ABBA – The Movie as its flip side. As there had not been a new single released by the group for eight months, The Name of the Game was an immediate success in Britain, entering the chart within a week of release, and two weeks later reaching Number 1 to become ABBA's sixth chart-topping single in three and a half years. It was a reflection of the Californian country/rock sound to which Björn and Benny were drawn, and there was at least one other track on ABBA – The Album which underlined their interest in bands like the Eagles.

Shortly before the release of The Name of the Game, a totally unexpected event occurred which came as a massive shock to Anni-Frid. The story of her birth to a German father had appeared in Bravo, a German magazine, which also related how her father had promised to return to Norway after the end of the Second World War, but had apparently perished when the ship that was taking him back to Germany had been sunk. The article, which had named him as Alfred Haase, was read by an ABBA fan in Germany, who had an uncle of that name, and she knew he had spent part of the war in Norway. Haase's version of events was that he knew nothing of Synni Lyngstad being pregnant, but had written a letter to her which had never arrived due to the chaos which the end of the war had brought. It also transpired that he had been married in Germany before serving his country in the war, and at the end of the war had returned to his wife and children and settled in Karlsruhe, close to the French border and not far from Stuttgart. It didn't take long before a tearful reunion took place between the father who could not speak Swedish and his daughter who knew little German, neither of whom had been aware of the other's existence.

Agnetha had other things on her mind, notably the imminent arrival of a second child for herself and Björn. She had bravely coped with the tour, the seemingly endless flights to and from Australia, the movie and everything else, while trying, successfully, to be a good mother to her daughter, Linda, who was nearly five years old when Agnetha produced a brother for her, Peter Christian Ulvaeus, on 4 December 1977. By then, all recording for the new album had been completed and it was decided to release it early in the New Year, allowing Agnetha to spend at least a little time with her new baby before the tiresome round of promotion restarted. Advance sales of ABBA – The Album in Britain had exceeded £1 million, guaranteeing it immediate platinum status. It was hardly a surprise, then, when it entered the UK album chart at Number 1, which was a far less frequent event than today, nearly 30 years later. It remained at the top for seven weeks, and was listed in the chart for well over a year.

The content of the album probably didn't much matter in view of the fact that it had sold so many copies in advance. Obviously, The Name of the Game would be included, as well as a studio recording of I Wonder (Departure); because this was one portion of the mini-musical, it made sense to include other portions, especially Thank You for the Music, and ultimately most of the second side of the album was a three part excerpt from The Girl with the Golden Hair, also including I'm a Marionette. In many ways, this was a brave attempt to produce something with a little more depth than simply a collection of pop songs, and the reviewer of the album in Rolling Stone magazine was moved to write: 'Side two is a real attempt to do something different, and, if not everything works, the effort is still laudable', although the British rock press were less positive, with the Melody Maker reviewer calling the mini-musical 'a mistake' and someone in Record Mirror rather foolishly writing 'This is where they come horribly unstuck', apparently overlooking the fact that the album had attracted over £1 million in advance sales even before the first punter had purchased it.

To some, the track which created most interest and controversy was the opener, Eagle, a song which, as mentioned before, was clearly influenced by, and also a homage to, the Eagles, the country/rock quartet which had emerged from California in 1971 to become one of the biggest acts in the world by 1977, although it is worth noting that the Eagles, at the time of ABBA – The Album, were far less commercially successful in most of the world than ABBA. The reviewer in New Musical Express, who plainly wasn't keen on ABBA or the Eagles, wrote that the song, on which Anni-Frid is a convincing lead vocalist, was 'a perfectly crafted pastiche of the Eagles' style, exactly capturing that sense of clinical blandness'. It should be remembered that the publication in question was a major supporter of punk/rock, and almost certainly negative towards most other pop and rock music styles. Another track on the album which was also in country/rock style was One Man, One Woman, which seemed to be about the break-up of a relationship, while Hole in Your Soul was another example of the group proving that they could still rock, and Move On, which begins with a spoken passage from Björn, was ambitious but probably a mistake, sounding somewhat dated. This leaves one other track, the second single included on the album, Take a Chance on Me. Like The Name of the Game, this single entered the UK chart within a week of release, and again like The Name of the Game, quickly ascended to the top spot, where it remained for three weeks.

In the USA, The Name of the Game had almost reached the Top 10 in February 1978, and Take a Chance on Me did even better, becoming ABBA's second ever single to make the Top 3 of the US chart, and also their second (and last, to date) million-seller. New Musical Express was much kinder about this song than they had been about Eagle, calling it 'one of those unstoppable eighteen line chorus songs which hold the secret of ABBA's success'. With two US Top 20 hit singles, ABBA – The Album became the group's highest placed album up to that point, peaking midway between Numbers 10 and 20, and also becoming their first platinum-certified album.

Two days before Take a Chance on Me reached Number 1 in the UK singles chart, ABBA – The Movie was premiered in London to a generally critical press reaction. Feminist magazine Spare Rib called the storyline 'the worst thing about the film', while the Sunday People reviewer wrote 'one forgets that this is virtually a 90 minute commercial (as) the overwhelming likeableness of ABBA is astutely rammed home', and The Guardian noted 'Everything is fine about ABBA except the film they have made. It is awful'

Anni-Frid and Agnetha on stage and in song

and the music press seemed to feel pretty much the same. Sounds suggested 'The Movie falls into nearly every trap ever laid for rock bands who attempt to cast their image upon the silver screen', and New Musical Express went further: 'This full-blown epic is shockingly bad, providing the ABBA fan with an embarrassingly feeble plotline to offset the preponderance of ABBA music'. Despite all the bad press, ABBA – The Movie was in the year's Top 10 box office hits, in a 12 month period which also brought Grease, Saturday Night Fever and Star Wars, which all produced better box office takings than ABBA – The Movie, although below ABBA – The Movie in the listings came such major hits and/or critical favourites as Woody Allen's Annie Hall, The Goodbye Girl (written by Neil Simon and starring Richard Dreyfuss) and The Stud (written by Jackie Collins and starring her sister, Joan Collins). It is hard to quarrel with some of the criticism attracted by ABBA – The Movie, and Benny's forebodings about ABBA's involvement with the silver screen seem accurate with the benefit of hindsight. The quantum leap from being a pop/rock star to becoming a big deal in the movie world is something many have attempted, but at which relatively few, even such a present day icon as Madonna, have succeeded for long. Ultimately, the only value represented by ABBA – The Movie is that it does show ABBA performing onstage, and while it was probably useful from the group's point of view in promoting ABBA – The Album, at least some of the quartet now probably feel embarrassed that they agreed to participate. Lasse Hallstrom, who had made ABBA's video clips, and was also given the job of directing the movie, can hardly be blamed for its shortcomings, as time was limited and outside elements, like the weather and the preponderance of outdoor shows, made his task far harder than should have been the case. Even so, the movie recouped its cost, which had been shared by Stig's company, Polar Music, and Australian media giants Reg Grundy Productions, a name many may recognise as also being behind such staples of daytime television as Neighbours, and the popular game show, Sale of the Century.

Stig Anderson's next task was to add the United States of America to the list of countries which ABBA had effectively conquered, and, in an attempt to achieve this, he agreed with Atlantic Records that they should jointly employ, at a cost of half a million US dollars, Scotti Brothers, a promotional company who had enjoyed success working with such clients as Barbra Streisand and

John Denver, as well as teenage idol Leif Garrett. A campaign lasting several months would include ABBA spending the last two weeks of April 1978 in the USA, which it was intended would be a perfect introduction to the proposed celebrations in May of an ABBA month – a whole month when the name and image of the group would be exposed widely across America.

In 1978 Ms Newton-John was one of the most popular and successful stars in the music firmament, with three Grammy Awards to her credit and a string of big selling singles and albums. Quite a contrast from when she was beaten by ABBA in the 1974 Eurovision Song Contest... 1978 was one of her biggest years, when she co-starred with John Travolta in the film musical Grease, which included several big hit singles, such as her duets with Travolta, You're the One that I Want and Summer Nights, and her solo hit, Hopelessly Devoted to You, which were all certified either gold or platinum. An important extra part of the Scotti Brothers promotion effort was a massive billboard on Sunset Strip advertising ABBA, which many regard as the pinnacle of an act's career – although it didn't do ABBA much good....

Also during May 1978 ABBA – The Album was certified triple platinum in Britain for sales in excess of £3 million, and, during the following month, a record dealer in Reading, Berkshire, was presented with the one millionth copy sold of ABBA – The Album. This was a hectic period for the group, and the activity wasn't confined only to the group, because Polar Music opened its own state-of-the-art recording studio in Stockholm which was primarily for use by ABBA, although it could be hired by others if the group were not using it. Among those who took advantage of the facility were Led Zeppelin, who recorded their 1979 comeback album, In Through the Out Door, at Polar, while Genesis members Mike Rutherford and Tony Banks also made solo albums at what was obviously a top class recording complex designed to allow ABBA to continue to make more of their music which had conquered a very large part of the world.

After a frantic few years which had almost certainly brought them fame beyond their wildest dreams, the four members of ABBA took a seven week holiday during the summer of 1978, which was their first lengthy break since before they formed the group. Before they left, Benny and Björn had written half the songs for the next ABBA album, although it would be nine months before it emerged. The group's attempts to fill the gap with more hit singles

The band in happier times

were successful, but only up to a point, as became evident with the arrival in September of the first single since Take a Chance on Me at the start of the year. One difference was that some parts of the lead vocal on Summer Night City were taken by Björn rather than one of the girls, and, more significantly, the backing was undoubtedly designed to be in disco-style, which was not well received critically. This was the first ABBA track recorded at the new Polar Studios, but it somehow lacked the magic of many of their previous hits and sales reflected this, although the single still made the Top 5 in Britain, becoming the first ABBA single in three years to peak outside the Top 3. In the USA, the single wasn't even released, because although Atlantic recognised its potential, ABBA could not guarantee that it would be included on an album available for that Christmas, and Atlantic did not want to release what they considered to be an obvious hit without a much more profitable album to follow immediately. In countries where the single was released, there was some controversy over what the girls were singing in the line before the repetition of the title, which was actually 'walking in the moonlight', but which some said sounded like doing something else, beginning with the letter 'f', in the moonlight. The song didn't really sound like the expected typical ABBA classic, as seemed to be confirmed by its chart position. The flip side of the single was somewhat of a surprise: a medley of well-known folk songs, which had previously been released on a charity album in Germany, Die Deutsche Krebshilfe. This throwback to the days of the Hootenanny Singers included Pick a Bale of Cotton, which had been a UK hit in 1962 for Lonnie Donegan, Britain's king of skiffle, On Top of Old Smokey, which had been a US Top 3 hit in 1951 for the Weavers, a classic American folk group which included Pete Seeger, and Midnight Special, also a Weavers hit, but from 1952, and a song which was also recorded by Lonnie Donegan. While Summer Night City wasn't as successful as nearly all of ABBA's recent singles in most of the world, it topped the chart in Japan, which the group visited in November 1978 for a promotional tour, which included a TV Special.

Shortly after this, in October 1978, Benny and Anni-Frid finally got married, although as they had been living as a married couple for several years, it made little difference to their situation. Their wedding meant that for the first time, the two couples in ABBA were both married, but, less than three months later, Agnetha and Björn announced that they were separating. With the benefit of hindsight, it appears that they simply had quite different priorities, with Agnetha preferring to stay at home and look after her children, while Björn was driven with a burning ambition for more success. The pressures of trying to live a relatively normal life while being an icon in the publicity-conscious world of popular music are something which very few marriages between musicians are able to withstand, as John and Christine McVie of Fleetwood Mac also discovered. However, that group wrote many of the songs on the incredibly big-selling Rumours album, which topped the US album chart for over 30 weeks in 1977 and was certified 13 times platinum, about the strain which success put on the relationships not only of the McVies, but also between Lindsey Buckingham and Stevie Nicks, while the remaining member of the band, Mick Fleetwood, was also divorced around the time the album was recorded.

However, the eventual break up within ABBA was by all accounts a massive benefit to the group, since it removed much of the tension that had built up between Agnetha and Björn, making it easier to work in the studio. Perhaps the private lives of the erstwhile couple after they split up are indicative of their different views on many aspects of life; Agnetha moved out of the marital home with the two children, while Björn quickly found a new girl friend, Lena Kallersjo, who was not involved in music, but worked in the advertising business. He later told those who asked him that he had only been a bachelor for a week, and that the bachelor lifestyle was not for him. More importantly for ABBA, Björn was able to concentrate on recording sessions for the next album, after a year when they had only released two singles.

There was another important item on the agenda for early 1979, when ABBA were one of a string of big name stars at a concert in the General Assembly Hall of the United Nations in New York to launch UNICEF's International Year Of The Child, hosted by the Bee Gees. Others involved included Andy Gibb, Olivia Newton-John, Rod Stewart, Kris Kristofferson & Rita Coolidge, who were still a married couple at the time, plus John Denver, Donna Summer and Earth, Wind & Fire, who were all brought in when both Elton John and Barry Manilow were unable to appear despite having agreed to participate. With compères David Frost and actors Gilda Radner and Henry 'The Fonz' Winkler, this extraordinary array of talent might well have been part of the inspiration behind Live Aid six years later. The show was filmed and later broadcast on television in over 70 countries, attracting a watching audience estimated at 300 million people. Apart from their live performance, ABBA were also generous in donating the music publishing rights to Chiquitita, one of the songs they performed, to the UNICEF cause, although it seems that some of the other participants were unwilling to do the same with one of their songs. Even when the multi-million selling Greatest Hits collection, ABBA GOLD, was released in 1992, the music publishing credit for Chiquitita in the CD booklet is listed as 'Music for UNICEF', and over the years, this donation must have raised a considerable amount for the charity. Later in the year, an album was released of music from the concert, but was barely publicised and managed only a month in the lower reaches of the US chart before vanishing, and missed the chart completely in Britain.

Having premiered Chiquitita at the UNICEF Gala, it was the obvious next ABBA single release, and appeared in late January. Another song with a Spanish sounding name as its title like Fernando, Chiquitita restored to ABBA the baton which appeared to have been stolen from them by British group The Brotherhood Of Man, who were also Eurovision winners in 1976 with Save Your Kisses for Me, and who had UK Number Ones in 1978 and 1979 with Angelo and Figaro respectively, although these songs, despite their titles being Iberian/Italian names, were lacking in the polish and brilliance of the ABBA songs. Chiquitita was the perfect way for ABBA to regain their position as probable chart-toppers after the commercially disappointing Summer Night City, and was also a very useful trailer for their next album, which was not complete at the time, but would emerge three months later. In fact, Chiquitita just failed to top the UK chart, as it was unable to displace Heart of Glass by Blondie, which was at Number 1 for virtually the entire month of February, and ABBA had to be content with being runners-up for two weeks, which must have resulted in a very acceptable donation to Music for UNICEF, as well as making it clear that, despite the marital break up, they were still very much in business. ABBA completists might be interested to learn that the flip side of the single, Lovelight, did not appear on any ABBA album until the 1994 release of the 4 x CD boxed set, Thank You for the Music, which included every ABBA single which had previously not appeared on an ABBA album, although when the ABBA Remasters series (of digitally remastered versions of each of the group's nine original albums) was released in 1997, both Summer Night City and Lovelight were included as bonus tracks.

Another trip, in February 1979, was to Switzerland for the filming of an episode of the BBC TV series, Snowtime Special, which produced groundless controversy because Björn was photographed talking to Liz Mitchell of Boney M, a group who were also in the show. British tabloid newspapers suggested that the two were romantically involved, which was a total fabrication, just as much as similar tabloid gossip about Agnetha having taken up with the marriage guidance counsellor whom she and Björn had consulted in an attempt to save their marriage. The truth was that Agnetha had continued to consult him after Björn had decided that he could see no point in further meetings, and Agnetha had visited the counsellor outside normal hours to avoid the paparazzi.   Chiquitita was the first hit in a year which must be counted their most successful of the period when ABBA were active as a group. In 1979, they accumulated five Top 5 singles (but no chart-toppers) as well as two Number 1 albums and also toured in North America for the first time, and

Britain (and other parts of Europe) for the final time to almost unanimous approval. Maybe this was the plan – let's all swallow our personal pride, and take advantage of the fact that we are one of the most popular acts on the planet. Just another couple of years, and we can all retire if we want.

Benny and Björn had spent time in both The Bahamas and Miami in Florida, writing songs and checking out studios, which led to them working briefly with one of the all-time great producer/engineers, the late Tom Dowd, who had previously worked with a veritable cavalcade of superstars: Otis Redding, Aretha Franklin, Cher, Dusty Springfield, Eric Clapton (Cream, Derek & The Dominos and solo), The Allman Brothers, Rod Stewart, Lynyrd Skynyrd, etc. Björn and Benny made it known that they would like to meet Dowd and watch him at work. Dowd, who was credited on the original Voulez-Vous album sleeve with 'help', explained: "ABBA were impressed with the nature of a pile of records that had come out of Atlantic Records, and they were interested in trying to put together an American rhythm section to try and make demos of several songs of a particular type. I was in California and they were on holiday in The Bahamas, and they called up Atlantic and said they'd like to go to Criteria Studio in Miami to see those rhythm sections you (Atlantic) talk about, and make a record with them. Atlantic was looking for me, but I wasn't there, so they used Ron & Howie Albert to put a rhythm section together, and they went in. I got back to Miami and my wife said 'ABBA are looking for you, they're up at Criteria right now', so I got back in the car and drove up to the studio. They were running through one or two songs and trying to experiment with the rhythm section, and I got on the floor and changed the parts, and changed the sequence and everything, and we made a good demo that day, and they wanted to come back the next day to rework that song and some other things, and we made two tracks for them the next day."

According to Carl Magnus Palm's ABBA – The Complete Recording Sessions (Century 22, 1994), backing tracks were laid down with an American band called Foxy for what eventually became the songs Voulez-Vous and Kisses of Fire as well as an attempt at If it Wasn't for the Nights, and all of these songs were included on the Voulez-Vous album. However, this was an experiment and what percentage of the recordings made in Florida remained on the released tracks is uncertain, but was probably very small. While Benny and Björn were on holiday, Anni-Frid had played an acting part in a Swedish movie, whose English-translated title was Walk on Water if You Can, which was filmed in Spain. When they all returned to Sweden, everyone concentrated on the new album, Voulez-Vous, which would appear in late April/early May.

Shortly before the album came another single, coupling two tracks which were included on the LP, Does Your Mother Know and Kisses of Fire. Despite the commercial hiccough which had occurred when Summer Night City had not featured exclusively female lead vocals, Does Your Mother Know was a song on which Björn sang lead, and like Summer Night City, Does Your Mother Know peaked outside the UK Top 3, even if it was just one place outside. Kisses of Fire sounded much more like the ABBA everyone knew and loved, and was much more recognisably ABBA, although its insistent disco beat was possibly overplayed to an extent. The single also became ABBA's first US hit in over a year, since Take a Chance on Me had become their biggest selling US 45. Does Your Mother Know was the ninth of their ten US Top 20 singles, while the album also peaked just inside the US Top 20 in a six month chart stay and was certified gold.

In the UK, the album went directly to Number 1, where it remained for four weeks during May and June, qualifying for instant platinum status which seemed to justify the fairly significant change in musical direction towards disco. Perhaps even more notably, five of the ten tracks lasted over four minutes, three of those over five minutes, and none was shorter than three minutes, emphasising the disco influence, but furthermore, many of the lyrics seemed much more adult than the previous pop-oriented simplicity which had permeated ABBA's work. By this time, Björn was feeling more confident about his lyrics, which tended to reflect the way he was feeling - that he was now separated from his wife - and could be relevant to his own situation as well as that of Agnetha. Also, Stig Anderson no longer had the time (and perhaps the inclination) to assist, as he was working behind the scenes on the world tour, which was scheduled to take place towards the end of the year.

After the relative disappointment of Does Your Mother Know, the next single, Voulez-Vous/Angeleyes, again coupling two tracks from the album, seemed somewhat of an improvement, as this started life as a double A-side, that is, with both sides of the single attracting interest, but after a couple of weeks, when the single entered the UK chart only just inside the Top 50, Angeleyes became the A-side. This produced further confusion and possibly affected the single's peak position – within the Top 3, but no higher – because Roxy Music had simultaneously released a single titled Angel Eyes, which was a different song entirely and whose title was two words rather than one. On occasions like this, both hits tend to lose out, and while the Roxy Music single also made the UK Top 5, both they and ABBA probably felt slightly cheated. Perhaps Voulez-Vous might have been a better choice for ABBA, but as this was also the title of the album, there might have been even more confusion…

At that point, half (five tracks) of the Voulez-Vous album had been released in single form, and three UK Top 5 hits had resulted. Of the other tracks on the album, the opener, As Good as New, started with an introduction by a string quartet before the disco-style backing which permeated the album. However, Agnetha's lead vocal suggested that the sound of ABBA was still just about present, while Anni-Frid's lead vocal, after a similar string-filled introduction, on The King Has Lost His Crown was an equally impressive performance on a vengeful ballad whose lyrics were seemingly allegorical and concerned the end of a relationship ('I believe your new girl turned you down'). This appeared to be much more personal than many of the group's previous songs. Anni-Frid also sang lead on the fairly frantic, but also fairly sexy Lovers (Live a Little Longer), another example of her thespian and theatrical inclinations. However, the slightly odd lyrics of If it Wasn't for the Nights were less audible, which repeated listenings do not seem to clarify.

If anything, Voulez-Vous was somewhat unsatisfying to these ears, although the inclusion of five hit singles (counting the title track and Angeleyes as two, despite their being the two sides of the same single) meant that the album was an inevitable success commercially, and an excellent launch pad for the forthcoming tour, which would result in the fifth and last hit single from Voulez-Vous. This was I Have a Dream, but, before it became the final hit of 1979, a brand new single, 'Gimme! Gimme! Gimme! (A Man After Midnight)' was a tour de force for Agnetha, to which her separation from Björn gave an added poignancy. This single reached the UK Top 3 while ABBA were on the British leg of the tour.

The 1979 tour, which would prove to be ABBA's final lengthy trek around the world, was a triumph, but in retrospect it is clear that performing live was not something which ABBA particularly enjoyed. The tour was planned for the autumn of that year, with over three weeks of dates in North America in September, followed by three weeks in Europe during October, but it had been decided in advance that the Far East and Australasia would not be part of it. This was partly due to Agnetha's insistence that she must not be away from her children for too long, but also because the only member of the quartet who was really keen on touring was Anni-Frid – both Benny and Björn preferred working in the studio to being onstage, where unexpected things could occur, no matter how well-rehearsed the show was.

ABBA around the time of Super Trouper in the late seventies

A special stage set was designed with an iceberg shaped backdrop coloured in blue, indigo and violet to represent the fact that ABBA came from Scandinavia, while the girls and Björn were dressed in figure-hugging Spandex costumes, although Benny opted out of these glam rock-inspired clothes. One problem which many acts would have welcomed, but which ABBA may have had to consider at length before it could be resolved, was which songs they should perform. With approaching twenty hits in their repertoire, and the need to perform a few additional tracks from the then current Voulez-Vous album as well as favourites like Thank You for the Music, song selection was one aspect that needed careful thought, as well as establishing the order in which the songs would be performed to provide contrast.

A nine piece backing band was assembled for the tour, which included four musicians who had also been on the 1977 tour in guitarist Lasse Wellander, Anders Eljas on keyboards, and a rhythm section of Rutger Gunnarsson (bass) and Ola Brunkert (drums), as well as another guitarist, another keyboard player and three backing vocalists. By all accounts, the Canadian and American dates went reasonably well, although it became clear to everyone involved that if ABBA were to add the USA to the list of countries where they were household names, it would require much more touring over several years, and this was not really an option, especially for Agnetha, who was hardly delighted to be leaving her children for this tour, and would probably have been even less happy if it happened again. As far as Canada was concerned, the group were already well known there, with several hits to their credit, which might well have been the reason for the North American leg of the tour starting in Edmonton, Alberta, where the 15,000 seat auditorium had sold out on the day the tickets went on sale, and the show at New York's Radio City Music Hall was also sold out, although some shows were less well-attended.

Around the time of the end of the North American leg of the tour, the new single, Gimme! Gimme! Gimme! (A Man After Midnight) was released, and was followed two weeks later by an album, Greatest Hits Vol. 2, which included ten tracks which had made the UK Top 5 as singles. Although most ABBA fans in Britain would already own most, if not all, the 14 tracks on the LP, it had attracted an advance sale of over 600,000 copies, which guaranteed it instant double platinum status. However, problems with manufacturing enough copies prevented it from entering the UK chart at Number 1 in its first week of release, but the following week saw it rise to the top to become ABBA's fifth consecutive chart-topping album – a perfect way to herald the European leg of the tour, which began on 19 October with shows in Sweden, Denmark, France, Holland, West Germany (this was prior to the unification of Germany), Switzerland, Austria and Belgium before arriving in Britain, culminating in six nights at London's Wembley Arena. The 48,000 tickets for the Wembley residency were put on sale five months earlier, and were all sold within hours of the box office opening.

One of the unexpected highlights of the 1979 tour came when the quartet performed I Have a Dream, probably the least disco-influenced track on the Voulez-Vous album, on which a children's choir joined in the chorus. No doubt it required considerable pre-tour organisation, but at each venue a local children's choir was on hand to provide the same sound as the recorded track, and when the tour was over a live recording of the song made at Wembley, with a flip side of a live version of Take a Chance on Me, also recorded at Wembley, was released as a single. On the picture sleeve, the group had written a dedication: 'November 1979 will always be full of fond memories of our UK tour. Releasing this single gives us the opportunity to thank the thousands of you who made our visit so memorable. In 1979, The Year of the Child, I Have a Dream had a special meaning for us and enabled us to perform the song with choirs of British school-children, who joined us onstage each night'. Released three weeks before Christmas, the single was an obvious instant hit, eventually peaking at Number 2 in the UK chart, and ending the decade on a high for the group.

A brief interview backstage at Wembley brought the following quotes from Björn: "Most people would say we've conquered the USA because our albums have gone platinum. If you consider the States conquered, then there's nowhere they don't play ABBA, except maybe China – but I don't think they have many record players there. If they had, they'd be playing ABBA." When asked whether a tour of Russia was likely, Björn said that the group had no plans to tour there, and that they were looking at the current world tour as a final tour "but we said the same about the last tour, and we're not calling this a farewell tour because we've seen the Rolling Stones do that several times." Benny, when asked why their earlier stronghold of Australia was not included in the 1979 tour, said: "Well, one reason is that it's a terribly long flight to Australia – 34 hours on the plane. If you don't feel you have to go there, it's pleasanter to stay at home. Not that we've done a lot of touring – since Brighton in 1974, we've only been on the road about 12 weeks in all, and that's not much. I do enjoy tours, but not all the travelling and the hotel rooms, and I certainly prefer the creative side of my work. It's much pleasanter for me to create music in the studio than to just reproduce it on stage." How long did they feel ABBA could continue? Benny: "I've no idea. I wouldn't dare make a guess. It's a matter of will and potential, wanting to do something. But I really enjoy what I do. Without work, life would be meaningless. It's the major part of my life." Björn: "I don't know how much longer we can go on, but we don't make any long range plans any more."

One aspect of ABBA's mission to conquer the world, as mentioned by Björn, was that, thus far, very little progress had been made in Spanish-speaking countries, but everything was about to change. Buddy McCluskey, an employee of RCA Records in Argentina, the label which released ABBA's records in South America, suggested that they should record one of their songs with Spanish lyrics, which he would write with his wife, Mary, and a Spanish version of Chiquitita had been released in the spring of 1979 and had topped the local chart, apparently selling half a million copies in Argentina and no doubt many more in other countries of that mysterious continent. Later in 1979, it was followed up by Estoy Sonando, a Spanish version of I Have A Dream, which was also a great success. As a result, someone suggested an entire album of ABBA songs with Spanish lyrics, and while Benny and Björn spent time back in the West Indies, this time in Barbados, in early 1980, writing material for the next album, Anni-Frid and Agnetha agreed to recording Spanish vocas on the backing tracks for ten of ABBA's songs. Some of them were well known, including Dancing Queen (Reina Danzant), Fernando, Mamma Mia (neither of which needed new titles) and Thank You for the Music (Gracias por la Música), which became the title track of the album, as well as lesser items in hit terms, such as Hasta Mañana and Al Andar (Move On from ABBA - The Album). Buddy McCluskey's idea was a great success, and the album, which was released in mid-1980, sold in significant quantities in Spain, Argentina, and for reasons which no-one seems able to explain, Japan. It was also released in Britain, where it unsurprisingly failed to chart, although it hardly mattered to Benny and Björn, who had shown little interest in the project, as it was the female voices that were the only change necessary for the Spanish recordings.

The songwriting expedition reportedly worked even more successfully than the previous year's Caribbean adventure, and five completed songs resulted, four of which would appear on the next album, while the remaining song, Elaine, became the flip side to ABBA's next single. However good Elaine had been, and it's OK, in a rather frantic way, it would have paled into insignificance in comparison with the song which became ABBA's next single, The Winner Takes it All, which is widely regarded as the finest single track ABBA ever recorded. With lead vocal by Agnetha, this was a song with lyrics by Björn in which the protagonist expresses regret that a romance has come to an end. When the media picked up on the apparent similarity between the song's lyrics and the break up of Björn and Agnetha's marriage, it was said that while Agnetha's vocal was absolutely perfect, she was only playing a part, as she had previously played the part of Mary Magdalene in a Swedish production of the Tim Rice/Andrew Lloyd Webber rock opera, Jesus Christ Superstar. Björn, who had written the lyrics to The Winner Takes it All, told journalists who asked whether the song was based on reality that neither he nor Agnetha had been the winner in their marital tragedy, although as recently as 2006 The Winner Takes it All was placed at Number 1 in a televised Top 40 chart of 'Break Up Songs'. This indicates that the sentiments expressed in the song remain true a quarter of a century after the song became one of ABBA's biggest and best-loved hits, restoring the group to Number 1 in the UK for the first time since Take a Chance on Me in early 1978, and also becoming their third and last US Top 10 single.

But before this excellent single was released, ABBA had taken their live show for a three week tour of Japan, where over 100,000 people watched the 11 sold out gigs, six of which took place at Tokyo's Budokan venue, where several rock acts, such as Cheap Trick, have recorded live albums. This turned out to be the last time ABBA ever toured as a group, and was also a period when tabloid newspapers were publicising Polar Music's non-musical activities, such as the story that they had been paid for records by exchanging them for a fully loaded oil tanker, which was said to have sunk, losing both ABBA and Stig Anderson substantial sums. According to Carl Magnus Palm's

Bright Lights, Dark Shadows, these details are incorrect, but the result was still expensive and large sums were lost. Palm also reports that ABBA and Stig made quite a financial killing on a bicycle manufacturer when exercise was trendy, but that wasn't reported because tabloid journalism was more interested in failure than success. One of ABBA's few mistakes was to ever admit that they had diversified outside music, and maybe another was to let it be known that they had lost money. The music industry in the early 1980s was fragmenting, and there seemed to be a feeling of schadenfreude towards ABBA's continuing success. The marital separation was another thing, provoking sympathy. The recording sessions which produced The Winner

ABBA walk through the fields during time away from recording

Takes it All resulted in one of ABBA's most shamefully overlooked tracks, Our Last Summer. With Anni-Frid singing lead, it's a joyful recollection of a woman recalling a summer in Paris with a football fan named Harry, with soaring vocal harmonies comparable with The Mamas & The Papas – an accolade for which only ABBA qualify, and maybe Spanky & Our Gang.

The marriage between Benny and Anni-Frid was also experiencing problems. They had been married for two years, but outside ABBA, had very different interests, and perhaps felt under pressure to maintain the group image of happy couples without the help of Björn and Agnetha. Perhaps fortunately, Benny was spending a lot of time in the studio with Björn, writing and recording the backing tracks for the other tracks on the album, which they decided would be called Super Trouper, which is also the name given to the huge onstage spotlights used by major rock acts.

The promotional video for the title track showed ABBA surrounded by circus performers – acrobats, clowns, animals – and it was originally planned that it should be filmed in London's Piccadilly Circus in the middle of the night, but the Metropolitan Police refused to allow it, fearing that central London would be over-run with ABBA fans hoping to be in the video, apart from which there is a ban on the use of circus animals in that area. The video and the sleeve photographs were eventually captured in a Swedish studio. The title song was one of the last to be completed, and was released as a single in Britain a week before the album, and after three weeks was Number 1, where it remained for the three weeks leading up to Christmas, when it was overtaken by John Lennon's (Just Like) Starting Over, which was dropping down the chart until Lennon's murder. The mourning only lasted a week initially, when St Winifred's School Choir's nauseatingly sentimental There's No-one Quite Like Grandma ruled the roost over the New Year period, after which Lennon returned, first with Imagine, then with Woman, before Joe Dolce took over for three weeks until Roxy Music's chart-topping cover Of Lennon's Jealous Guy.

The Super Trouper album didn't mess about, going immediately to Number 1 in the UK charts, and staying there for nine weeks. Apart from the two Number Ones and Our Last Summer, it included a couple of tracks, Lay all Your Love on Me (the UK Top 10 single following the title track) and On And On And On, which became disco favourites. The Piper, which was also the flip side of the Super Trouper single, was basically a musical rewrite of the story of the Pied Piper of Hamelin, but was perhaps also a warning to the people of Europe (and the world) that a charismatic individual like Adolf Hitler might return if politicians did not pay attention to prevailing circumstances. Andante Andante is a love song, and the repeated musical term of the title means gently or slowly, while Me and I, with lead vocal by Anni-Frid, deals with schizophrenia, not an obvious topic for a song by ABBA, and the lyrics include a reference to Dr Jekyll & Mr Hyde, although the subject matter does not result in a track listeners should avoid. The two remaining songs on the original album were both somewhat sentimental: Happy New Year is self-explanatory, with a singalong chorus suitable for seasonal pantomimes, but once again, the song's lyrics emphasised that there had been a change in the chemistry of the group, while The Way Old Friends Do, which was recorded live during the 1979 Wembley concerts, and seemed to confirm that things had changed for ABBA, but that they might attempt to soldier on: 'I don't care what comes tomorrow, We can face it together, The way old friends do'.

While ABBA's career was going from strength to strength commercially, the relationships between the two erstwhile married couples were proceeding quickly in the opposite direction. Björn and Agnetha were divorced and in January 1981, Björn married his new girlfriend, Lena Kallersjo. Later that month, the quartet were reunited for one day to celebrate Stig Anderson's 50th birthday, which Benny and Björn marked by writing a song for the man who had masterminded ABBA's ascent into international stardom, but this is not a song most ABBA fans are ever likely to hear, as only 200 copies of the song, Hova Vittne, whose title translated into English is Hova's Witness, were pressed as red vinyl singles. February brought more bad news for ABBA fans, as Benny and Anni-Frid announced that they were divorcing.

Benny remained fairly content with his life in music, although Anni-Frid, whose life had been considerably more complicated, had inevitable feelings of great insecurity, although it seems highly unlikely that she was experiencing financial difficulties. Benny found a new girlfriend, a television reporter named Mona Norklit, and moved out of his marital home, a villa on the exclusive suburban Stockholm island of Lidingo, to live with Mona in an apartment in the city itself. Benny, whose greatest interest and joy involved making music, was soon working with Björn on songs for the next ABBA album, the follow-up to the multi-million selling Super Trouper, which was apparently regarded by the group members as their best album thus far. The apparent curse of both living and working with your spouse, which had already affected Björn and Agnetha, as well as the various members of Fleetwood Mac, clearly still applied. However, it must be said that ABBA never quite produced from their marital strife an album as commercial and which provoked such critical inspection as the British and American band's Rumours.

In April 1981 the quartet were the subject of a TV Special titled Dick Cavett Meets ABBA, in which the celebrated American TV personality came to Sweden to film an interview with the group members, which would be interspersed with live performances of songs covering much of ABBA's career, including a couple of new songs which ABBA had only just recorded. Nine songs in all were performed, and this informal concert completes the audio/visual part of this package. Inevitably, a number of hits were performed, including Gimme! Gimme! Gimme! (A Man after Midnight), Super Trouper, Knowing Me, Knowing You and Summer Night City, as well as comparatively rarely heard songs from the Super Trouper album like Me and I and On And On And On. The two songs from the forthcoming album attracted some interest; Two for the Price of One is an extraordinary song about a man seeing an advertisement in a lonely hearts column, and being rather surprised when he discovers that instead of the one woman he is expecting to meet, her mother is also part of the package. The listener might be tempted to ask for a pint of whatever Björn was drinking when he wrote those lyrics... The other new song was more serious and a much more accurate reflection of the real life dramas which were affecting Björn and Agnetha in particular. Slipping Through My Fingers was about the passage of time, and Björn was apparently moved to write the lyrics when he saw his daughter, Linda, going to school one day, and felt, like many parents in similar circumstances, that he might have been so busy becoming a pop star that he had neglected to notice that his children were growing up. The TV Special also included the by now inevitable Thank You for the Music, and while some critics felt that Dick Cavett's interviews with group members were less than revealing, the performances of some of these songs surely must rank as unique.

The first track to be heard from the forthcoming new album was One of Us, which could be termed a typical ABBA track, apart from the fact that its lyrics dealt with the end of a relationship. With lead vocal by Agnetha and an unstoppable chorus, this was bound to be a hit, and indeed it was, reaching the UK Top 3, and probably not making it to the very top due to the date it was released (three weeks before Christmas 1981), which meant that it had not gathered quite enough momentum to overtake the best selling single of the year, Don't You Want Me by The Human League, which remained at Number 1 for five weeks, and also Cliff Richard's revival of the Shep & The Limelites doo-wop classic, Daddy's Home, which was at Number 2. Nevertheless, the sound of One of Us augured well for the new album, which appeared a week later. Its flip side, Should I Laugh or Cry, appeared as a bonus track on the ABBA Remasters series CD reissue of the album, which was titled The Visitors. Should I Laugh or Cry is a rather bitter song which seems to be about, unsurprisingly, the end of a relationship when one partner becomes aware of the shortcomings of the other partner, after being unable to see them when the relationship started due to tunnel-visioned love. Perhaps the reason it was not included among the original nine songs on the album is that it is not a happy song, although it is performed very well.

ABBA's ninth and last original album appeared two weeks before Christmas 1981, and entered the UK chart at Number 1, where it remained for three weeks before it was overtaken by The Human League's Dare, which spent virtually the rest of January at the top. A new ABBA single was released in early February, Head over Heels, which was also included on the chart-topping album, perhaps resulting in this becoming the first new ABBA single in a long time, in fact six and a half years, to peak outside the UK Top 10. Not only that – it didn't even make the Top 20! It's a strange song about a woman in a failing relationship who tries to remain cheerful by shopping and making herself feel rich and important, and perhaps anyone who bothered to listen carefully to the lyrics found it somewhat inaccessible. The flip side of the single was the title track of the album, and The Visitors was another song hardly typical of ABBA, recounting a story about someone waiting for an inevitable visit by someone who would 'take' them and 'break' them, which seemed rather sinister, and indicates that Björn's songs were becoming political, as the only possible identity of the visitors was the police. Or perhaps soldiers, which is the title of another track on the album, which seems to be about how the military are unlike other people, with the slightly odd chorus line 'soldiers write the songs that soldiers sing'. This wasn't a bright and cheerful ABBA album like its predecessors, and many of the tracks seemed cold and efficient rather than warm and welcoming. Perhaps one exception might be the resigned but partially optimistic When All Is Said and Done, while the closing track, Like an Angel Passing Through My Room, is not a happy song as the protagonist reflects on past situations and people in tones of regret, as a ticking clock can be heard throughout the song.

Even the sleeve picture of the four group members seems rather odd: the group are in what looks like a hotel lounge, and Agnetha stands on the left reading a book, while Anni-Frid sits in an armchair in the centre of the picture. Björn, looking glum, stands with his right arm leaning on a chair, and Benny looks relaxed. There is no feeling of closeness about the picture - none of the quartet are looking at any of the others, and only Benny, seated on a chair, seems to be looking at the camera. Perhaps the remaining track, I Let the Music Speak, is suggesting that after all the good times and bad times, music will never let you down, and, like several other songs here, sounds far more like a song from a theatrical presentation than a pop song. Of course, the next big thing which involved Benny and Björn was the musical Chess, on which they worked with the British lyricist, Tim Rice, as their collaborator...

Overall, The Visitors was a disappointment, both commercially, as it only remained in the UK chart for less than half the time that Super Trouper had managed and only included one big hit single, and aesthetically, because the majority of the songs seemed pessimistic, which, of course, they were. An era was drawing to a close for ABBA, and each of the four members would have to prepare for life outside the cocoon in which they had lived together for much of the previous ten years.

Anni-Frid was the first to strike out on her own with a solo album. She had made two previous solo albums before the ABBA years, Frida in 1971 and Min Egen Stad in 1972, as well as another one in 1976, Frida Ensam (Frida Alone), which was produced by Benny and topped the Swedish album chart for several weeks, and included a version of Fernando sung in Swedish that became so popular that it was re-recorded as an ABBA song. Other songs on Frida Ensam included versions of 10cc's Wall Street Shuffle, the Beach Boys classic, Wouldn't It Be Nice, and Charlie Rich's The Most Beautiful Girl in the World, and, for her new solo album, Anni-Frid selected Phil Collins, then a member of progressive rock group, Genesis, as producer. She had heard the Collins solo hit, In the Air Tonight, and had also listened to his 1981 solo album, Face Value, which had topped the UK album chart, and apart from enjoying it was also interested to learn that it had been recorded at a time when Collins was in the midst of a divorce from his wife. He seemed like an obviously sympathetic producer for Anni-Frid, who was also just divorced. The album was titled Something's Going On, and what was its first single and effectively its title track, I Know There's Something Going On, was written by Russ Ballard, an Englishman who had written a number of hits, such as Hot Chocolate's 1977 UK Number 1, So You Win Again, and Rainbow's 1979 hit, Since You've Been Gone, and was also a member of the group Argent, led by Rod Argent, an ex-member of the Zombies. Rod Argent himself also contributed a track to Anni-Frid's album, Baby Don't You Cry, on which the horn section of US group Earth, Wind & Fire guested. Anni-Frid's favourite track on the album was apparently a Giorgio Moroder composition, To Turn the Stone, although perhaps the most interesting track was Threnody, more a poem than a song. The title means funeral song, and it was written by the famous American satirist Dorothy Parker, and set to music. Released in the latter half of 1982, both the album and the first single charted on both sides of the Atlantic. The album briefly made the UK Top 20, and peaked just outside the US Top 40 during a six month plus chart visit, and the single almost made both the UK and US Top 40s.

Benny and Björn were still interested in another original ABBA album, and two brand new tracks, I Am the City and Just Like That, as well as a lesser track, You Owe Me One, were recorded possibly for that album, but after all the divorces and attendant media attention they decided to delay it for a year and instead release a double album which would include all the hit singles, as well as a couple of new tracks, perhaps the two already mentioned. In October 1982 a new ABBA single, The Day Before You Came, was released. This failed to grab the attention of UK record buyers, and peaked just outside the Top 30, and, in fact, an English synthesizer duo named Blancmange covered The Day Before You Came in 1984, and their version peaked ten places higher than the ABBA single. The double album, logically enough titled The Singles – The

First Ten Years, was released in November, and included one track which had not been heard, Under Attack, or perhaps two, if So Long is counted, as this was the only ABBA single which had failed to make the UK chart. It didn't take long for the album to become ABBA's ninth consecutive UK Number 1, which almost certainly ruined the chance of Under Attack doing well, as it was included on the chart-topping album, but even so, the single reached the UK Top 30. The two singles and The Day Before You Came's flip side, Cassandra, were actually the final ABBA tracks recorded. The ABBA story appeared to be over.

In 1983 Agnetha made a new solo album. She had previously made nine solo albums in Swedish, but this one was to be aimed at the world market. After apparently asking Barry Gibb of the Bee Gees to produce, but finding him as unwilling to leave Miami, where he lived, as she was unwilling to leave Sweden, she eventually settled on Mike Chapman, an Australian who had experienced considerable success as one half of the Chinnichap team. With his partner, upper crust Englishman Nicky Chinn, they had written and produced hits for the Sweet, Mud, Suzi Quatro and others, but Chapman alone had produced a string of hits for Blondie and was seemingly pleased to be asked to do the same for Agnetha. Unfortunately, he was less successful with Agnetha Fältskog than with Deborah Harry, although three singles, The Heat Is On, Wrap Your Arms Around Me (the title track of the album) and Can't Shake Loose, all made brief visits to the UK chart without reaching the Top 30, although the last of the three, which was written by Russ Ballard who had also written Frida's biggest hit, crept into the US Top 30. The album, on which three members of the group Smokie (another hit act produced by the Chinnichap team) supplied most of the backing vocals, briefly reached the UK Top 20 and peaked just outside the US Top 100, but many of its world sales of over one million were in Sweden, where it topped the chart, as had The Heat Is On.

After recording was completed on the few new ABBA tracks for the double LP, Benny and Björn started working seriously on the Tim Rice project. Lyricist Rice had been responsible, with tunesmith Andrew Lloyd Webber, for such theatrical triumphs as Joseph & His Amazing Technicolour Dreamcoat, Jesus Christ Superstar and Evita, and he was now interested in writing a musical which was perfectly described by Carl Magnus Palm as 'the game of chess as a metaphor for a love story, as well as the East-West relationship during the cold war years'. Despite Björn's growing confidence as a lyricist, the idea of working with a proven master of the theatrical musical brought for Benny and himself the possibility of writing something which would be appreciated by a much wider and more demanding audience than ABBA's relatively simple pop songs. Following the way both Jesus Christ Superstar and Evita had been launched, Chess appeared initially as a concept album (in fact, a double album), for which Tim Rice (with some assistance from Björn) wrote the lyrics and Benny and Björn the music, as well as assisting in the production of the recording.

The basis of the story seems to have been inspired by a 1982 world chess championship which took place at a hotel in Iceland between the Russian champion, Boris Spassky, and Bobby Fischer, representing the USA. For the Chess musical, Rice conceived the quite fictitious plot that a woman who was part of the American presence had fallen in love with the Russian champion, which unsurprisingly upset the latter's wife. The part of the Russian champion was played by Swedish vocalist Tommy Korberg, and the part of the American player by Murray Head, a British actor who had played the part of Judas in Jesus Christ Superstar, while acclaimed Scottish singer Barbara Dickson took the part of the Russian's wife, and Elaine Paige, who seemed to regard Tim Rice as her patron, was the American woman. The soundtrack recording (as it was called) was released in November 1984 and included two substantial hit singles. One Night in Bangkok by Murray Head, made the UK Top 10 and the US Top 3, while a duet between Barbara Dickson and Elaine Paige, I Know Him So Well, topped the UK singles chart for a month in early 1985. This latter success allowed Benny and Björn to join a highly exclusive list of producers who had been responsible for ten UK Number 1 singles. The Chess double album remained in the UK chart for four months, peaking just inside the Top 10, and spent a little longer in the US chart, reaching the Top 50. However, this success was not mirrored when Chess was staged in London's West End and on Broadway in New York. In London, it staggered on for three years, largely recouping its cost, but in New York, after one particularly negative review, it closed after two months. It is probably fair to say that the story line was simply inappropriate for a musical, but at least it included a couple of hit singles...

Both Agnetha and Anni-Frid continued to make English language solo albums, which they hoped would be internationally recognised. 1984's Shine by Anni-Frid was produced by Steve Lillywhite, who had also worked with Peter Gabriel, U2 and others, but it charted for a single week in the UK and not at all in the US, while 1985 brought Agnetha's Eyes of a Woman, produced by Eric Stewart of 10cc, which reached the UK Top 40, but was also ignored in the US. Anni-Frid at that point decided to give up music and devote herself to her new lover, a German prince named Ruzzo Reuss. Agnetha made two Swedish language albums, in 1986 and 1987, the latter with her son, Christian – she had made an album with her daughter, Linda, back in 1980 – and also in 1987 tried for a third time to make an English language album, this time with producer, Peter Cetera, the erstwhile lead vocalist of the 'brass rock' group, Chicago. I Stand Alone included a minor US hit single, a duet with Cetera titled I Wasn't the One (Who Said Goodbye), but was only a genuine success in Sweden, after which Agnetha also distanced herself from music.

In 1985 and 1987, Benny and Björn produced albums for a Swedish brother and sister duo, Anders & Karin Glenmark, whose albums were released under the name of Gemini. While both albums reached the Top 20 of the Swedish chart, that was virtually the extent of their success. In 1987 Benny also launched his own record label, Mono Music, and recorded a solo album of Swedish folk songs with the wonderful title of Klinga Mina Klockor, which translates, as might be expected, as Ring My Bells. Although hardly commercial, and not designed as such, it reached the Swedish Top 10 and sold well over 150,000 copies, while a 1989 album by Benny, appropriately titled November '89, also did well. In 1990 Agnetha had married for a second time. Her new husband was a surgeon named Tomas Sonnenfeld, but unfortunately the marriage failed to last and ended in divorce in late 1992

Björn and his family had moved to live in England during the mid-1980s, and it seemed that the whole ABBA affair had drawn to a conclusion, especially with the release in 1986 in Sweden of ABBA Live, a live album consisting of tracks recorded on both the 1977 and 1979 tours, as well as the nine tracks recorded for the Dick Cavett Meets ABBA TV special. The album didn't fare too well, even in Sweden, and it wasn't released in the UK until 1992.

1992 was the year when what might be termed the ABBA revival occurred.

A rare less than flattering publicity shot of the band

In 1989 Stig Anderson had sold Polar Music's publishing catalogue, which included ABBA's songs, to Polygram for a reputed sum of nearly £30 million. When the deal had been done, it transpired that Stig had failed to honour an agreement he had made with Benny and Björn in 1984 to increase the royalties they received. Stig's excuse was that the agreement had been made on the understanding that ABBA would continue to record new material, although the group members denied that any such condition had been mentioned. Eventually the group members sued Stig's company, Polar Music, for over £2 million, and the case was settled out of court for an undisclosed sum.

In 1992, Erasure, the duo of Vince Clarke (synthesizer) and Andy Bell (vocals), recorded an EP titled ABBA-esque of cover versions of four ABBA hits, Lay All Your Love on Me, SOS, Take a Chance on Me and Voulez-Vous, which topped the UK singles chart for five weeks. Around the same time, an Australian band known as Björn Again became the first and best of numerous ABBA tribute bands. It is said that the reason the tribute band syndrome occurred was because the various genuine articles had made it clear that they would never perform live again, and Australia, in particular, being a long way away from the rest of the pop/rock world, would never have the chance to see ABBA play live, so tribute bands sprung up for acts like the Beatles – the Bootleg Beatles were probably one of the first tribute bands – Led Zeppelin, the Rolling Stones and ABBA. The first prerequisite was for the tribute band to sound like the act to which the tribute was being paid, and the second, although less important in the scheme of things, was that they should physically resemble and dress like the original act. Björn Again have been active for probably 14 years, and are still a very popular act booked for tours as the opening act for the Spice Girls (at Wembley Stadium), Nirvana (at the Reading Festival), Shania Twain (on a nationwide UK tour) and others.

Coincidentally, the various international licensing agreements for ABBA's recordings had all ended in 1992, so that Polygram Records, which now owned the ABBA catalogue as a result of purchasing Polar Music from Stig Anderson, could release a Greatest Hits compilation all over the world without needing to ask anyone's permission. The result was ABBA Gold Greatest Hits, which was released in late September 1992. A 19 track album, it contained all nine ABBA UK Number 1 singles plus ten of the group's other biggest hits, the only exception being Thank You for the Music, which had come to be recognised as the group's signature tune. The album topped the charts in Australia, Austria, Denmark, Germany, Ireland, Israel, Italy, Mexico, Portugal, Singapore, Spain, Sweden, Switzerland and the UK during its first two months of release, and, by the first day of 1993, it had worldwide sales of over four million copies and had been certified platinum in 19 countries.

About one month before the album was released Anni-Frid had married the German prince, Ruzzo Reuss, with whom she had been living for some time. She also became very interested in environmental issues and saving the planet, although her musical involvements were few at this point. Also just before ABBA Gold appeared, Bono, the leader of the hugely successful Irish group, U2, invited Björn and Benny to a U2 concert in Stockholm, and they joined U2 onstage for a version of Dancing Queen, while the late Kurt

Cobain, of the American group Nirvana, made it a condition of his band playing England's Reading Festival in 1992 that Björn Again should also be on the bill. Various other 1990s acts, including REM, the Fugees and others, performed ABBA songs, and even Pete Townshend of the Who reportedly said that SOS was the best pop song ever written.

The success of ABBA Gold had continued to the point where sales exceeded ten million copies (and subsequently, it has topped 15 million!) Obviously, ABBA had not been forgotten in the ten years that had passed since they were last active, and inevitably there was discussion about a companion album which would include all their other hit singles, as well as a selection of album tracks which it was felt deserved more attention. More ABBA Gold – More ABBA Hits was released in May 1993, and, although it failed to equal its predecessor in topping the charts, the album performed very well commercially, reaching the UK Top 20 and eventually selling over two million copies.

More unexpected promotional assistance came from Australia, where two 1994 movies, Priscilla, Queen of the Desert and Muriel's Wedding, featured ABBA music, and meanwhile Benny and Björn had started work as far back as 1990 on another musical, this time based on the famous novels written by Wilhelm Moberg about early Swedish settlers in the USA during the latter part of the nineteenth century. Eventually the completed musical, whose Swedish title was Kristina fran Duvemala, was staged in 1995 and fared very well in Sweden, although it seems unlikely that it would be able to attract interest outside Scandinavia.

Anni-Frid released a new solo album in 1996, Deep Breaths, produced by Anders Glenmark, one half of the Gemini duo who had worked with Benny and Björn, and it was a success, topping the Swedish chart, while shortly afterwards Agnetha released a double CD compilation, My Love, My Life, covering her entire career, which even included a few ABBA songs, but this was less successful. However, 1997 brought bad news when Stig Anderson, who had managed ABBA through their musical conquest of virtually the entire world, died at the age of 66.

The premiere of a theatrical musical titled Mamma Mia! took place on 6 April 1999, coincidentally the 25th Anniversary – to the day – of ABBA's Eurovision triumph, and used many ABBA songs, but was very definitely not biographical. The bizarre story is hard to explain, but clearly the main aspect of the show's popularity revolved around those familiar songs, which are quite cleverly interspersed in the show. This musical has been performed in many parts of the world ever since its first appearance, and has generated vast amounts of money for those involved, which is deserved as Mamma Mia! has become one of the most 'hot' tickets in London's West End, and at the time of writing is still booking more than six months in advance.

Coinciding with the start of the Mamma Mia! musical, ABBA Gold returned to the top of the UK album chart for five more weeks during the spring of 1999, proving that ABBA's music was enduring and could cross generations in much the same way as Elvis Presley, the Beatles and maybe the Rolling Stones and Bob Dylan. It is difficult to imagine a greater compliment…

In their own words

Interviews with Anni-Frid Lyngstad, Pip Williams, Hugh Fielder and Rod Liessle

ABBA were a pop phenomenon. Formed in Sweden by Björn Ulvaeus, Benny Andersson, Agnetha Fältskog, and Anni-Frid Lyngstad, under the watchful eye of manager and mentor Stig Anderson, the quartet released their first single in 1972 under the cumbersome name of Björn and Benny, Agnetha and Anni-Frid. It was Anderson who coined the catchier acronym ABBA, and European success soon followed.

Although the band's first stab at Eurovision glory missed somewhat (1973's 'Ring Ring' was dismissed for Swedish selection), in 1974, 'Waterloo' stormed to victory, subsequently topping charts Europe-wide.

Despite the commercial failure of their first two albums, taking their respective names from their two Eurovision entries, ABBA's climb back to the top began with the release of 'S.O.S.' in August 1975, quickly followed by the number-one success of 'Mamma Mia' and their eponymous third album.

An incredible succession of international hit records followed, as ABBA sold records in the kind of volume not seen since The Beatles. Like that group, ABBA had a distinctive sense of style, appeared in their own feature film, and were eventually broken up, after seven years of unprecedented pop success, by creative and personal tensions.

The ABBA legacy is still very much with us – tribute bands like Björn Again tour the world constantly, while Ulvaeus and Andersson are currently working as producers on a film version of Mamma Mia, the hugely successful stage musical based on their songs.

These interviews offer a concise and insightful analysis of ABBA's music and subsequent influence on popular culture, and feature contributions from Björn Again founder Rod Leissle, famed English record producer Phillip 'Pip' Williams, and former Sounds journalist Hugh Fielder, as well as from Frida herself.

Leissle is the co-manager and sometime bass player of Björn Again, the tribute band that he started with his friend John Tyrell in 1988. Since then, the band have broken out of their native Australia and toured the world, playing at the Reading Festival in 1992 at Nirvana's request. Leissle and Tyrell have now franchised the Björn Again name, and there are currently five different incarnations of the band playing worldwide.

Williams has worked with such luminaries as Dame Shirley Bassey, Carl Douglas, and Barclay James Harvest, and is most well-known for producing Status Quo's defining album, Rockin' All Over The World, in 1977. He is a confirmed ABBA fan, and actually shared a studio with them in '77 when they were rushing to finish 'The Name Of The Game'.

Fielder has written for British publications Sounds and NME, among others, and continues to be an active music writer, offering his intelligent views on such diverse artists as Cream, Genesis, and The Police.

Here, the three discuss ABBA's music, focussing primarily on their hit singles, and dissecting the song writing, the production, and the way the songs were performed live.

Pip Williams: We didn't know what had hit us when ABBA came on the scene for the '74 Eurovision song contest with this song, 'Waterloo'. They were very shrewd because they realised that for a European group to gain worldwide appeal, the only route for them then was Eurovision, so the song was written specifically for that show, and where a lot of the Eurovision fodder was quite typical, quite formulaic at that time, 'Waterloo' was a breath of fresh air.

Hugh Fielder: They took Sandie Shaw's 1967 Eurovision song contest winner 'Puppet on a String' and they basically updated it, making sure that it crossed all international boundaries, and that there was something in it for everyone. Ring Ring, their debut album, had been very much a formative record – influenced by late Beatles and early Elton, with a Phil Spector-ish production. It contains their first single, 'People Need Love', which was a Brotherhood-of-Man-style piece. The album isn't terribly distinguished, although the title track gives you a clue to ABBA's character; with the dense production and the unique use of the voices you can see some of the elements that would go into classic ABBA songs later on. The other thing that 'Ring Ring' has going for it is a very clever minor-key twist in the chorus, again one of those elements that ABBA would use more and more later on. They also brought in Neil Sedaka, who at that time was a very successful pop singer and song writer, to do the lyrics for the song. I think that pointed Björn and Benny to the kind of ideas that they would develop later on. There are a couple of what you might call lost ABBA songs on that album. 'Honey Honey' is one of them – it's perhaps the first time that you become aware of the character of the voices.
Rod Leissle: I think that 'Waterloo' was successful at Eurovision because they took some interesting subject matter and played around with the concept, producing an amazing song in the process. The outfits they wore were amazing; I don't think that anyone else would have dreamt up those clothes in a month of Sundays, so I think that they married together a whole bunch of things to win that competition, and I think they just outshone everyone else that day.

The way that they approached the contest was incredible. They had it set in their sights, they were going to win, and there was no question about it – it was that self-belief, but also the ability that went with it; it was just great.
HF: At that point they were still just a slightly sophisticated pop band; they hadn't really developed the elements that would make them the group that they became. Funnily enough, I think that 'Ring Ring' probably shows more about the 'true' ABBA than 'Waterloo' does. 'Waterloo' was really purpose-built to win Eurovision, and in that sense it did its job really well.
PW: Although it didn't have the stamp of later ABBA, it certainly hinted at what was to come, with the lovely, plunky piano sounds, and the saxophones, later revisited, of course, on 'Does Your Mother Know'. It was a jaunty song,

The group relax on the beach

they looked great, and it was so un-Eurovision at the time – it just had to succeed, and of course was a number-one single in the UK. It's not typical of some of the deeper material that they did later, but certainly if you now revisit it and go back you can see that the germ of the whole ABBA sound was definitely there. It's actually a little bit cleverer than you think. It was a nice angle for a lyric: "You've Met Your Waterloo, You've Met Your Match". One wonders what the French thought of it at the time! I think that a lot of the charm was in the fact that they sang in English. No European groups who sang in their mother tongue were very successful – it was another shrewd move to sing all of the songs in English. After all, who could resist their wonderful accents – "I feeel like I ween when I loooose" – it was just unbelievable. There was a charm in hearing these lovely girls singing with that accent. That was just another piece of icing on the cake for me.

HF: On the early singles, like 'Waterloo' and 'Ring Ring', it's impossible to tell the two voices apart. They're singing the same notes, just doubled up, so it's a dual vocal without overdubbing, and you've got that live tension of the two voices together. Later on, they develop this idea, and one of them could subtly change the tone of her voice, seemingly changing the whole pitch of the two voices, so that you'd get subtle shades within what was just basically singing in unison. Because of the two characteristics of the two voices it always sounded like there was far more going on. Frida's voice was slightly lower, and had a slightly more distinctive edge to it than Agnetha's, but Agnetha was, at the same time, able to mimic other vocal styles much better and bring a more dramatic quality.

They didn't actually write any of the music themselves, but they brought to the whole idea of pop vocals something that more experienced female singers like Barbara Streisand and Liza Minelli actually didn't have, because, in a sense, they were too sophisticated. Agnetha and Frida brought with them a simplicity, plus the subtle difference between their own voices, to make something that was quite dramatic in that sense. Benny has said that ABBA songs wouldn't have sounded the same if they'd been using two other girls and I can't think of any other girls' voices that would blend quite as cunningly, and create quite such an effect.

PW: 'Waterloo' was short, under three minutes, and it said all that it needed to say in that short amount of time, so it was actually a masterful pop song.

When I play it, to this day I listen and I'm thinking, actually they knew exactly what they were doing. They were craftsmen, they were real craftsmen.

HF: Neither of ABBA's first two albums really had much impact outside Sweden, apart from in Germany maybe. They were the first singles band in that sense; the singles were far better than most of the tracks on the albums! It wasn't until later on that their albums started to achieve a more uniform quality, and therefore spawned more hits. The first two albums only have two, maybe three hit singles, but later on they were pulling five or six singles off the album.

PW: 1975's 'SOS' definitely set up the whole ABBA phenomenon. It was a quirky 130-something beats per minute, and there was no computerized click-track, so there was human lulling and acceleration built into the tempo; it felt like a clock mechanism ticking over, and again it was irresistible. The vocal harmonies in the chorus were absolutely brilliant, and there was more than one hook. A lot of pop songs tend to have just a verse, then a hook, then a bridge; ABBA songs at this time were full of hooks – you'd hear the chorus, and then you'd hear that lovely section "How can I/Even try/To go on", which becomes the outro, like another chorus.

RL: It starts off as a bit classical, I guess Bach induced – a link between the ballad and the rock song – and then you're in for a really powerful chorus. 'SOS' is great; you've got three musical styles all glued in together there, I think it works great.

HF: It's a slightly strange arrangement in many ways, one that allows Agnetha's voice to add quite a passionate vocal to it, but what's also interesting is that the piano and synthesiser are used to carry lines in the song that would ordinarily be done by the voices, so that the voices and the instruments become intertwined.

PW: It was also the start of the incorporation of alliteration into the lyrics and the titles – 'SOS', 'Mamma Mia' – and the assonance which of course crept into a lot of the other songs: "Dancing queen/young and sweet only seventeen/feel the beat from the tambourine". They would go for these nagging rhymes that would just drill themselves into your brain. Of course, it wasn't a new thing, alliteration had been used in many 50s pop songs by countless artists, and it was like ABBA had delved into pop history to find all of the ingredients for success. Alliteration was just one of them.

Importantly, here was a song title that was catchy in itself, setting the trend for all of their hooky titles. It reached number six in the UK, which, while not quite climbing to the heady heights of later singles, set the scene for 'Mamma Mia', and that incredible run of number ones. I loved the keyboard playing on it – very, very classical in influence, with those flowing arpeggios – it showed that these guys were not just like the manufactured reality TV-show acts you see today, that Benny and Björn were fantastic musicians and that they could craft the most intricate musical arrangements. The two ladies were trained singers. These were not girls that were plucked off the streets, and they'd had pretty substantial solo careers themselves before ABBA.

HF: It may be low-key during the verses, but when it gets to the chorus there's a whole phalanx of acoustic guitars crammed in, and the voices are rather compressed, so it gives you that rather distant feeling; they seem to recede, having been quite close to you for most of the verse, to allow other bits and pieces to come in, and again, it just keeps you hooked.

PW: 'SOS' was the catalyst for what was to become a phenomenon. Here was something that was immensely commercial, but still intensely musical underneath it all, and I think that this was a vital secret to their worldwide success. It wasn't pap, it wasn't puerile, and it wasn't twee. 'SOS' was really the first single that hinted at something beyond the four attractive people on stage.

'Mamma Mia' was a number one in December '75, three months after the success of 'SOS'. It was a fantastic song, with a fantastic alliterative title. Again, it had all of the elements we'd come to expect from ABBA, and there were hooks all over the place. It was prior to the real ABBA disco era, it was before 'Dancing Queen', but it was still a track that you would dance to at a Christmas party.

RL: 'Mamma Mia' is a great example of just getting a lyrical hook, one that sticks once you hear it, and you hear the rhythm that goes with it. It's just a great combination of rhythm and lyric and melody, you know; it's a classic ABBA pop tune.

HF: I think that 'Mamma Mia' is the first glimpse that we got of what you might call ABBA genius. It starts with that piano and xylophone intro, like it's going to be another Eurovision hit; then the voices come in and take it somewhere else. It's very cleverly done – the voices build up, and the whole song thickens up until you get to the chorus, when it breaks down again. The chorus is very well constructed; the first repetition is quite naked, there's nothing there, and the second time there's just a single string note running underneath the voices. That single note builds tension, which then is released in the last part of the chorus, satisfying the listener with a wonderful sense of release – ahhhhh. That's clever. The whole song is stuffed full of little musical ticks and devices that they now feel brave enough to use. It's certainly the most ambitious song they'd attempted up until then.

PW: The vocal arrangement is just stunning. It's quintessentially European; you can't imagine anyone in the UK coming up with a record like 'Mamma Mia', although lots of ABBA copy groups came along and tried to replicate the formula later on. It had 'number one' stamped all over it. 'Mamma Mia' was also their first UK number one since 'Waterloo'. They'd had a couple of less successful intermediary singles, which proves that they were probably just feeling the ground and trying to find the right formula. Another group that I love is Del Amitri, who always manage to find a hook within the song title, and the most successful ABBA songs had a hook within the song title – 'Mamma Mia', 'Take a Chance on Me', and so on – this was the first of many.

HF: The words became a part of the song, part of the rhythm of the song. They were very clever at that – tying the words themselves up with the rhythms of the songs. The title is its own little rhythmic phrase all by itself, and they built on that musically.

'Hey, Hey Helen' [from the same album, 1975's ABBA] was a glam rock ABBA, and employed that same alliterative trick. There were a lot of glam elements in their music, but they took the style and used it in their own way. 'Hey, Hey Helen' is still fairly derivative, they hadn't quite got there yet. It's a song they played in 1975, in their live set. In fact, I think they used it to open the show. They never played that show in England, and, in fact, by the time they came to England the song had disappeared from the set. At that point nobody was really buying ABBA albums, so it was really something of a lost song.

RL: It's one of the songs that the fans talk about a lot. We [Björn Again] have done it, in the UK years ago, and it worked well, but because it is not one of the quintessential ABBA songs, it's not a regular fixture of our set. I don't think it was really indicative of ABBA. I think that they were more about the melodies, and the music that they were known for wasn't really the rockier stuff. I mean, 'Hey, Hey Helen' is pretty raunchy.

HF: 'So Long' is another glam-rock-influenced song. ABBA hadn't really developed their glam style as yet, and this could easily be a Sweet song, or even a Suzie Quatro song. It's okay, just not really distinctively ABBA, and there was much better to come.

RL: It's a track that works really well when Björn Again play it in concert; it's really up, and goes into a kind of swing feel. That's a bit of a hallmark for ABBA as well; they do shuffles and swings and stuff like that. It's got a bit of an edge to it, too; there are some interesting effects in there. I think there's one particular effect, at the start. They got a slide and drew it all the way up the guitar strings, right to the very top, and they overdubbed it several times. It's a weird kind of effect which they distort, and they marry that with a vocal technique as well, so it's got those studio things happening. 'So Long' is another great rocky song of theirs. I think it's probably them trying to sound rockier, to get away from the pure pop label that they'd acquired.

HF: To be honest, it doesn't really do them justice, on their own terms. It showed that they could do a reasonable glam rock song – they were to pick up a few fashion tips from that lot – but they had more to offer.

'I Do, I Do, I Do, I Do, I Do' [Their next single] is often regarded as something as a flop for ABBA, because it didn't actually make the charts in Britain, but it was a hit pretty much everywhere else around the world. Certainly in Australia, which actually turned out to be a more devoted ABBA Land than almost any other country, it became a particular favourite. In fact, I think it was the one that Muriel walks down the aisle to in Muriel's Wedding.

RL: I think that the song works because it has got a very straightforward melody which works over quite furious instrumentation. There is a lot happening in there, but it is very much a sing-along song because the melody is quite simple. It was a different feel as well, a kind of shuffle. I think that it was typical ABBA in that it was quite original. I can't imagine that too many other bands would have come up with a song like that.

HF: It's a tribute to a 1950s band leader called Billy Vaughn. It has that wonderful opening saxophone line, and then when the voices come in, it's the first time you get those two girls' voices bathed in echo, struggling to be heard above the chiming bells, the clanging pianos, the xylophones, and everything else going on around them. Then it just explodes into the chorus and suddenly the whole ABBA technique is laid out there in front of you. I mean, it's a pretty silly song one way and another, but it does the job perfectly and is identifiably ABBA now. We know what we're getting; this is fun pop music. Still, it's not generally considered amongst ABBA's biggest hits because it wasn't a hit in England, but it was a hit almost everywhere else around the world. For that reason, you won't find it on ABBA Gold; you have to go and look for ABBA Gold Vol. 2.

PW: 'Fernando' was a number-one single in March '76. The Abba version was actually its second incarnation; it appeared earlier on a solo album by Frida [her 1975 Sweden-only release, Frida Ensam].

HF: It was originally a rather plain boy-meets-girl story, and now suddenly they're a bunch of Mexican revolutionaries reminiscing over their youth. Just to make it slightly more plausible – which you might need, with them coming from Sweden – they put the whole song onto a sort of blanket of South American pipes and those acoustic guitars – I suppose it goes along with the hats, really, doesn't it? – and the whole thing develops into a rather kitsch Latin American thing that only ABBA could get away with.

PW: 'Fernando' remains a firm favourite of mine because it's just so gentle.

Abba in the early eighties, a changed look from their early careers

When you listen to the verse, you're sitting 'round a fire, wrapped up in a blanket, and then the huge chorus comes in.

HF: 'Fernando' does lay on the whole Latin-American thing a bit thick at times, but then that's ABBA's skill, to be able to do that without really getting you to take it seriously. You don't actually think these people really come from South America; for a start, they're all a bit too blond, aren't they?

'Dancing Queen' is probably the most-played ABBA song on radio, or indeed in dance halls. It's the perfect combination of voice and instruments. They get it absolutely spot on at this point, and the two dovetail together perfectly. Again, you've got all these little tricks; the voices build up and then suddenly diminish. When you listen to the line, "having the time of your life", the voices are lowered slightly in the mix, so that you're leaning forward to hear it, just before the chorus breaks. It's another one of those cunning tricks from Björn and Benny, who by now knew exactly what it was that would turn the audience on.

RL: I think it's great - the vocal range goes from the very bottom to the very top – and then some if you listen closely. There are definitely some sped-up vocals; I can hear Frida screaming in some kind of weird falsetto, right at the back of the mix, but you can definitely hear it in there. So it's the whole vocal range. The piano hook is a key to it as well: derdum, derdum, derdum. That's the great thing about ABBA; when you need the right hook, if it's a lyrical hook, something you can sing along to, or a musical hook, there's always something in a song that you can relate to, and it anchors the track. It shows off the girls' vocals too. They're singing in unison, and then they will break off and go into the harmonies in the choruses.

PW: That fabulous plodding beat meant that on a dance floor you could dance to it in half time; you could have a slow dance with your partner or you could have an up-tempo disco dance. It was unbelievable, the power of the thing when you first heard it on the radio. John Lennon even made the comment that he was astonished at the sheer power of 'Dancing Queen', and that's high praise indeed!

The vocal sound was just wonderful. They employed some technical tricks that actually pummelled the song into your brain. They used this box called the Aural Exciter, an electronic gadget that exaggerated the high harmonics in the voice. If you listen to those lines, "young and sweet/only seventeen/oh yeah", and the "dancing queen", you can hear this long repeat echo that gets thinner and thinner and thinner, a very glassy tone caused by this device. When you listen to it on the radio, these high harmonics just embed themselves into your brain! It was a technique that they employed a lot. It was an irresistible sound, and 'Dancing Queen' was arguably their first disco hit.

HF: Björn and Benny were looking for something more like the disco sound that they'd been hearing in America. It's a bit more laid-back than that, but it still works.

RL: They seemed to focus on the disco stuff because they could see that there were a lot of people out there writing disco, and it was getting a lot of airplay.

PW: They preceded the Bee Gees by a year, and they realised the power of the clubs. One can look at the story as it developed on the gay scene, in the gay clubs. When you think about gay anthems and gay icons, you're talking about Shirley Bassey, ABBA, and Kylie, of course, later on. The song was incredibly intoxicating when it first came out. I was playing the ABBA Gold album again only last night. You put 'Dancing Queen' on and you want to play it again. It's that groove – 101 beats per minute. A lot of the early singles were done without a click track; the tempo was humanised. You're not led by this absolutely metronomic beat, because it's got soul and it lives and it breathes. That track will forever be in my top five all-time greatest pop singles.

HF: 'Dancing Queen' is very 70s-sounding, because disco music is very 70s-sounding. Still, it does seem to be permanently retro. I mean, it doesn't matter how far you go on from the 70s, people always go back to that one. I mean, isn't that why cheesy discos exist in the first place?

PW: 'Money, Money, Money' came along in November '76, after 'Dancing Queen', and provided a big contrast to that song. With every subsequent single there was a different flavour. This time there was an Eastern European thing, with the wonderfully dark descending bass lines. I think that if Liza Minnelli had sung this song in Cabaret, it wouldn't have sounded out of place; it conveys this dark, mysterious mood. The bass playing on it is absolutely monumental, and probably one of Rutger Gunnarsson's best lines.

It's very theatrical. The video was a huge send-up, satirical of course, deliciously ironic because they were stinking rich at the time. There's a slight rocky influence from time to time, alongside this Eastern European feeling. That was the broad appeal of ABBA, that they could draw on so many outside influences. They could go from something totally different, like 'Fernando', and you could still say, "Oh yeah, that's ABBA."

RL: The rhythm in the verses is very special. It works incredibly well as a song, and it works especially well for us in a live context. I think it's the way the song builds through the verses and into the chorus, which is killer. It's interesting in that the kick drum drives the rhythm in the verses, the snare comes in just at the right place, and then the whole thing takes off with the chorus. The construction of the song is excellent.

HF: 'Money, Money, Money' is built out of a four-to-the-floor beat and a wildly infectious chorus. It also shows off Frida's voice. Frida always sang slightly lower than Agnetha, although you can't always tell because of the way the voices were blended; it was quite uncanny. Benny's arrangements are quite stagy, and for the first time you get the feeling that ABBA are looking more towards the songs as live-performance pieces, rather than just creative records. Perhaps it's the beginning of the next stage of the band, where they're beginning to think more in terms of stage production rather than studio production.

PW: In February '77, another song from the Arrival album reached number one: 'Knowing Me, Knowing You', later, of course, popularised by Alan Partridge. It was a fantastic song and it showed a darker side, a more mature side of their song-writing. This song is actually quite depressing, "In these old familiar rooms children would play/Now there's only emptiness, nothing to say", yet they still managed to make it sound like just another ABBA pop song.

HF: 'Knowing Me, Knowing You' is the sound of ABBA beginning to grow up. It's based on American pop, which Björn and Benny were becoming increasingly intrigued by.

PW: They were now able to create a sympathetic atmosphere to the lyrics. Now, this may seem like stating the obvious, but there's a particular part in the song towards the end of the chorus where they sing, "Knowing me knowing you/It's the best I can do", and then that very melancholic guitar line comes in. It conveys a sense of resignation, of, 'oh well, this is the best we can do.' The whole timbre is so well thought out. Each instrumental line complements the lyric perfectly.

RL: There are some great keyboard sounds in there. Benny was the master of coming up with the perfect keyboard sound.

PW: They incorporated all of the elements that we'd come to expect from ABBA. There are these fantastic harmonies, and when the chorus kicks in, it finds another gear, and the wonderful accents again! I love the way that Scandinavians have trouble singing 'Z's when it's actually an 'S', so you hear the line "Tearz in my ice" instead of "Tears in my eyes". I remember having a discussion with one of the girls from Björn Again, and I asked her, "Do you actually rehearse the charming little differences in the accent?" and she said, "Oh, absolutely. It's hugely important that you sing 'tearz in my ice' and not 'tears in my eyes.'" I'll always remember that whenever I listen to 'Knowing Me, Knowing You'; it's the whole package – a fantastic track.

'The Name of the Game' was a number one in October '77, but only in the UK and Ireland, believe it or not. Even in their beloved Australia, it only got to number six. It's a number-one single with me – absolutely my favourite ABBA track. It's so intricate musically that a musician has to love this particular track.

HF: This is ABBA starting to look at emerging mega-groups in America, like Fleetwood Mac and the Eagles, and adapting a lot of those techniques to their own flawless production style, creating something slightly grander than we'd been used to while still maintaining the same distinctive ABBA style within a slightly broader context, broadening out the vocals and the whole sound, I suppose you'd call it a widescreen sound, as opposed to the small, television sound that we'd been getting before, as it were.

PW: Whereas a lot of pop songs will have an intro and a verse and a chorus, maybe a middle eight then a fade out, this has five distinctive sections that are all so unbelievably accessible. You've got this moody, ploddy groove in the verse, then this lovely little pre-chorus section, "I was an impossible case", and then you get into the chorus, then the post-chorus, and the Frida-led breakdown, yet it never ever sounds cluttered, and it never ever sounds bitty. Five separate hooks in one song! All of them work together to make a masterful, cohesive whole. It's just a masterpiece, a sonic and a vocal masterpiece. For me, it's the pinnacle of their work – maybe not the most jaunty single, but fantastic nonetheless. Yet another wonderful lyrical idea, about a female patient who goes to her psychiatrist and falls in love with him. I mean, where were their heads at?

RL: 'Take a Chance On Me' is a great song, one that works really well for Björn

Again. It's one that the crowd really want to sing, and it's just got a great beat. Again, I wouldn't say that it's disco-y, and it's not rock. I suppose we've just got to say that it's pop, but it's great, and again, there's a great vocal thing happening at the start of the song. The chant that the boys are doing and the melodies that sit on the top of that chant set the song up. I understand that Björn wrote it when he was out jogging, and the rhythm of him running along the footpath gave him that rhythm – and it figures!

HF: I think that it's a classic example of ABBA using the rhythm within the words. The whole song is based around the rhythm of the words. Right from the beginning, the backing vocals build up and you've got layer upon layer of voices all just saying, "Take a chance, take a chance, take a chika-cha-chance". That's the basis of the song. On top of that, Agnetha is producing these breathy, sexy lines to go with it, to monumental effect. The instruments are almost irrelevant at times, because the voices provide the rhythm.

PW: The repeated chorus line motors the song along and keeps it moving with a constant sense of motion. It's got a brilliantly danceable groove, with that lovely galloping synth-bass line. The harmonies are unbelievably intricate and so well done, and it's full of synth licks and synth hooks. There are hooks everywhere, within the bass line, within the vocals, within the synths, and even as the song's fading out there's yet another hook. Every time you stop to breathe there's another hook that comes in, and yet it never sounds cluttered; it's just an unbelievably joyous song to listen to. Of course, there was darker stuff to come.

They were able to employ wonderful technical tricks to drive particular words and particular lines home. When they sing, "It's magic", all of a sudden they introduce this fizzy, crisp vocal sound that just pokes those two words straight into your brain. A lot of credit must go to the engineer, Michael B. Tretow. He was a master, and he was always at their side, always working with them to devise new electronic tricks, new sonic miracles, if you like, to drive home the wonderful sound of those voices.

HF: 'Take a Chance on Me' is really where the voices take over for one song. They provide the rhythm, the backing, the momentum – almost everything about it – and the fact that the lyrics don't actually mean a great deal is irrelevant by the end.

RL: I think that 'Summer Night City' is a great song. There's a great Moog

The girls put passion into their performance

synthesiser line which goes through the chorus, and that's the bit that I listen to. It's a bit like a solo, a bit like a keyboard solo which is happening at the same time as the chorus is going on. There's a great disco-y beat going on as well; it's got all the hallmarks of a disco-pop classic.

HF: This time, they'd been very influenced by the Bee Gees' vocals, because of course the Bee Gees were huge at this time with Saturday Night Fever. Again, that influenced ABBA, and ABBA turned it their own way.

'Chiquitita' [their next single] is a mixture of soft Latin rock and classical influences, blended together with subtler R&B influences. By now, ABBA were getting quite sophisticated at what they do and you can hear different strains and different styles running through the songs, because they're confident that their own style will pervade.

RL: It's a power ballad, I guess. From a musical point of view, it's a really strong song, one that gets to massive oompah status by the end. It's another song that works really well for us live, too.

PW: Another number-two record, with yet more complex sonic architecture, and more sonic textures. You have this lovely Mexican feel, and yet the end of it goes into an almost French thing, a kind of Les Miserables stomp. Again, all of the ingredients for a massive hit record were there. You had the plaintiveness of the verse, which makes you feel a bit melancholy, and then this uplifting chorus. I think it is just irresistible, and it's surprising that it wasn't a number one. I think that maybe they were trying to appeal to the Latin market. They'd absolutely conquered the world, and knowing how shrewd these guys were, it could possibly have occurred to them that the South American/Latin market was another huge market to conquer. Maybe that's just me being cynical!

'Does Your Mother Know' appeared in '79, just after 'Chiquitita'. By ABBA standards it was comparatively unsuccessful – it only got to number four – but it had a rock feel that harped back to 'Waterloo'.

HF: It came from a very firm rocky base, rather than the disco beats they had been using in the past couple of years, so it gave it a slightly different direction. Certainly the vocal arrangements in the chorus are among the best ABBA ever achieved.

RL: It's very mechanical and driving, and, again, there's a great lyrical hook, "Does your mother know you're out?" which I think is something that's very sing-along-able.

PW: Arguably, it might have worked better if the girls had sung it, but I think that it was time for a change, and the fact that it still was a top-five single shows that the public were prepared to embrace any sonic changes that ABBA were going to throw at them, even if it meant a lead vocal from Björn as opposed to Agnetha. The subject matter – it's about an underage girl – is a bit risqué, and it was just a stopgap in a sense, but I think it has a valid place on the ABBA Gold album. It's a great single, and any other band would be proud to be associated with it, even though it doesn't have the sparkle of some of the other things ABBA produced.

'Voulez-Vous' was a number-three record in August 1979, and obviously cashed in on the disco renaissance which the Bee Gees started a couple of years earlier. It's tailor-made for the market; blitzing brass lines and plodding fours at 120 bpm. They even incorporate the obligatory breakdown towards the end, when it goes round and round and round. Every disco record had to have a breakdown where you went right down to the bass and the drums. It's a fantastic track, it really is, and markedly heavier than their earlier pop singles like 'Dancing Queen'. The whole sound of it, although it's still ABBA, smacks of that Bee Gees thing from 'Staying Alive'. I'm sure that they were cashing in, but why not? They realised that they could sell ABBA singles in the dance clubs, and that the clubs were becoming very, very popular. I'm sure that 'Voulez-Vous' was written specifically for the disco market and nothing else.

HF: 'Voulez-Vous' came out sometime after Patti LaBelle sang 'Lady Marmalade' and used the, "Voulez-vous coucher avec moi?" line. It probably stuck in Björn or Benny's head at some point and got retrieved and recirculated, in a completely different way, of course.

RL: The hooks and the brass stabs and the chorus I think are typical ABBA things; you came to expect to hear those things during that period. I think in many regards they were giving people what they really wanted – great songs, really sing-along-able choruses, and great rhythms to dance to, as well.

HF: 'Gimme, Gimme, Gimme' is probably ABBA's best disco track. It was quite calculated as such, and you can tell from the arrangement that they are being very deliberate about it. It's a very calculated build-up in terms of the arrangement, the instruments, and then the voice. Every part fits together.

With other bands it would seem too contrived and constructed, but with ABBA it just seems to flow very naturally, and Agnetha certainly gives one of her raunchiest performances.

RL: It's really well-produced, and there is a marriage of disco in the verses, with the octave bass line, and rock in the choruses. It's a great combination of the two together.

PW: Erasure did a great cover of this [on their 1992 EP Abba-esque], and it was probably significant that ABBA were starting to absorb the emerging electro influences. Their previous singles had had more traditional instrumentation, and now they were incorporating more synth sounds. 'Gimme, Gimme, Gimme' again used that alliteration in the title, and was much more solid as a disco song, but had all the ABBA trademarks as well – swirling synth lines, a great hook, and stunning vocal harmonies. I constantly wonder at the complexity of the vocal arrangements. Two girls off the street could not have handled that. The vocal prowess of these two ladies was obvious, and they were able to handle anything that Benny and Björn threw at them.

One has to mention the great string arrangements on this track. The guitar arpeggios in the intro are fantastic, and then there is this big moody string line that descends into a droning cello riff. One mustn't underestimate the importance of all the guys that work with them, from Michael B. Tretow, who produced on a lot of the singles, to Anders Eljas, their co-arranger. I think they'd be the first to acknowledge the contribution of the guys behind the scenes.

HF: There was a great cover of 'Gimme, Gimme, Gimme' by a Swedish industrial metal band, Beseech. They took the rhythm and gave it a really metallic edge, and the vocals were turned very low and given a very sort of aggressive, macho stance, which of course took it beyond camp into something quite sinister.

'The Winner Takes It All' actually revitalised ABBA's career at the start of the 80s. There's no doubt that the vivaciousness that had come so intuitively to them in the 70s was starting to sound jaded. Also, by now, the band were no longer two couples, and the splits were beginning to show. There was a tendency for people to start reading into ABBA lyrics at around this time, for the reasons why they broke up, the heartbreak and everything else, and perhaps this song explores some of those issues. Benny claims that he was pissed when he wrote the lyrics, and he was certainly feeling a bit down at this time. His soon-to-be-ex-wife certainly gives one of her better vocal performances on it. What you want to read into that, who knows? To be fair, ABBA kept themselves to themselves when it came to that, and while obviously many of the lyrics from this time allude to the splits that were happening between them, nothing could be really construed as personal.

It is certainly one of the better songs from their later era. It's very well constructed; the grandiose piano introduction, the dramatic vocals that Agnetha sings, the combination of the two vocals, the production techniques are all very well-practiced, well-versed, but somehow it seems to lack the intuitive vivacity that ABBA always had. Perhaps this is ABBA trying to be more controlled, trying to be more sophisticated – perhaps too sophisticated.

After all, ABBA were a great pop group, and pop music doesn't stand a great deal of sophistication. If you want to get sophisticated with pop music, then you should probably go off and perform another style, but by now ABBA were really condemned to being a pop group. It was how they were going to be remembered, and there was no chance of them developing another style. This song probably takes them as far as they can go without them becoming over-sophisticated, without losing the point of what a pop band is supposed to be about.

PW: If you talk to ABBA fans, then this is the one that they really love and that they really relate to. Whether or not the fans could perceive it at the time, there was obviously a huge change coming in the thing that was ABBA.

RL: I think that it's astonishing that they made a hit song about something that is so heart-rending and personal, but that typifies ABBA, in that they wore their hearts on their sleeves with a lot of their songs. It's a great song with incredible production in the studio, and I think it's the one song that we find very hard to do in Björn Again, because the production is so hard to emulate on stage, and that puts it in a bit of a special place for me. I think it's possible that it's one of my favourite songs.

PW: It's about that feeling of resignation again: "Okay, we fought, we had a battle of wills, but I lost, and the winner takes it all". It's a real tearjerker and it raised feelings in everyone that's ever had a relationship break-up. It's a funny thing, there is a commerciality in tragedy. I'm sure that there are people that are almost sadistic in the way that they love a song that actually makes them cry. People that have been through relationship break-ups will be triggered by the merest sentimental hint, the merest melancholy line, and ABBA were shrewd to exploit this.

What is bizarre is that they were prepared to put out a lot of their down songs, which are so obviously about their personal experiences, almost like airing their dirty laundry in public, if you like. I know quite a few acts that would not even consider releasing singles about such deeply personal matters, but 'The Winner Takes It All' was a number-one single, and is still immensely popular. I can see people covering this song for years to come. It's got an Edith Piaf melancholy about it, and quite rightly has its place in the canon.

RL: It's very Phil Spectorish, just a wall of sound coming at you and, without that kind of studio stuff happening I think it's very difficult to make it work in a live sense. The song still stands up; it's a great song, but people remember that wall of sound, especially when you get to the chorus, and without that the song can possibly fall a little bit flat.

HF: Actually, ABBA were never that much of a hit live. The myth has kind of grown up in retrospect because I think they only did two or three world tours, if that, and not that many people saw them. ABBA: The Movie showed them in a pretty good light, but they weren't that strong a stage act, because obviously they couldn't reproduce all the studio nuances of their hits. So they rather bounced around, pretending to be much more approachable and audience-friendly, whereas the thing about ABBA in the studio was that you had this glorious, almost cloying studio perfection to their songs. They still managed to keep their distance. In fact, like all the best pop groups, you're better keeping your distance. When you try and be too audience-friendly, you just end up being entertainers, which is fine, but you lose the mystique.

RL: Obviously, ABBA were sensational in the studio. It's a given that they were just amazing, and everything was so pristine. So could they do it in a live sense? I believe that they could. They were a brilliant band. I never saw ABBA live, so I can only reference ABBA: The Movie and the concert that they filmed at Wembley. The concert at Wembley was incredible. Their live set was awesome. They'd got the best production, the best people to play on stage, and it was just so exciting. I do think that Björn was a little bit frightened of presenting ABBA in a live sense, given that they had done such amazing stuff in the studio, but I think that they really delivered.

The kind of sound that they produced in the studio with Michael B. Tretow was a Phil Spector wall-of-sound kind of thing, and so there were guitar overdubs, loads of vocal overdubs, and tricky techniques with flying vocals in vari-speed – all these kinds of tricks that they were doing in the studio, so how did they emulate that on stage? It was pretty much power of numbers, so if there were three guitar overdubs in the song, they would get three guitarists up on stage to do it. It was the same with backing vocals. There were always three or four people doing BVs at an ABBA gig, 'cause in the studio, the girls did loads and loads of overdubs, so you needed that vocal strength there on stage.

I think that the disco songs worked extremely well for them on stage, and that is reflected in Björn Again. When we do a gig, we put those songs towards the end of the set, when people are really going for it! I think that they worked very well for ABBA in a live setting.

Still, the version of 'Dancing Queen' that they did at Wembley stadium was – not great. I don't know what got into them that day, but if you listen to the tempo, it's ridiculous, over 130 beats per minute. If you listen to the studio version it's about 102 beats per minute; the song just completely changes rhythmically, and the feel is lost. I'm sure that they listened to it and thought, "Oh my God, what happened there?" In this day and age, just about every drummer works to a click track with a tempo map attached to keep them on the straight and narrow, and it keeps a song where it's meant to be in terms of rhythm and timing. I think, perhaps, back then maybe the drummer got overexcited – but the tempo was way, way too fast, and unfortunately they did not do the song any sort of justice at all.

When they toured Australia in '77 they made a documentary about their tour, which later formed part of ABBA: The Movie, with a great director in Lasse Hallstrom, and given that it was an incredible tour there were some great gigs, great audiences, and great direction to pull it all together. It turned into a mini masterpiece. Okay, it's not the greatest film on the planet, and not many people really actually know about it, but I think it's a bit of a mini masterpiece, so that's one of the highlights of ABBA for me.

HF: By Super Trouper, it's becoming clear that ABBA were no longer having the time of their lives. They're no longer two couples, and there's a weariness

The passion of the live performance was clear to see

about it, as well. The title of the song is interesting. The Super Trouper was one of the huge stage lights that was used to highlight the group on their world tour, so the chorus, "Super Trouper lights are gonna find me", is really about the band trying to avoid the spotlight; for the first time in their career they're looking to get out of the spotlight rather than into it. By this point ABBA had stopped touring. They'd stopped touring after their second world tour. The 1980 tour was the last one they did, after which they retreated back to being a studio band. They'd never really become a hugely successful live band. It would have taken more effort and more professionalism to turn them into that, and to get huge stadium-style audiences on a regular basis – and by now I don't think that the will was there. There was a will to keep writing the songs, but the performances became something more wearisome, I think.

PW: Two divorces and the rigour of touring, always having to appear smiling and full of vitality for the press and the public, must have taken its toll on them.

HF: It doesn't stop it being a very fine song, however. It's very well constructed, as always, and they turn the world-weary edge to their own advantage. It has a kind of pristine quality that pulls you in. You certainly don't get downhearted listening to it. You don't feel a weariness listening to it. You don't feel, "Oh, here comes another ABBA song!" They've still got that ability to pull you in. It's just that you can tell – perhaps for the first time – that they are beginning to admit to themselves that their life as a pop group is not going to last forever.

PW: When she sings, "When I spoke to you last night from Glasgow", it sounds to me like she's singing, "When I spoke to you last night from Tesco's". I think that Björn Again might use those words in their version.

RL: Even just from a musical point of view, it's a great track. I think that it has got some really interesting rhythms in there, brought about by a synth bass that underpins the whole track. I don't know what instrument it was played on, I think it was a Jupiter 8, but it creates a fantastic basis for this sort of song. It's just one of my faves.

HF: The Super Trouper album was largely written in Barbados by Björn and Benny. Going away to write an album had worked for them earlier on, but this time they seemed to be running a little thin on ideas. The production was also a bit muted, which meant that when they were not actually on sparkling form it could quite easily slip into a rather bland formula, which by now was beginning to take them over.

They no longer really had the sparkle because the intuitive sense had gone. I suppose that the sheer joy of creating music that was so successful had now passed and they were now expected to produce that kind of music constantly. Actually, they weren't necessarily feeling like that as people; as people they had become more reflective. After all, they had a lot to reflect upon, one way and another – what success had done for them as a group, as individuals. Bits and pieces of that occur in the songs. Again it's not direct; it's nothing you can pin on any one person, but the elements are there.

PW: Significantly, 'Super Trouper' features Frida on lead vocals, as opposed to Agnetha, which gives it a more mellow sound. Agnetha is a soprano and Frida is a mezzo soprano, which leads to the wonderful blend between their two voices and their great harmonies. The track is fabulously constructed, as are all of ABBA's songs, again with wonderful synth hooks and that oom-pah groove which some people think is a little bit puerile. I happen to think that it's a great groove.

'Lay All Your Love on Me' also came from the Super Trouper album, and was a relative flop by ABBA's standards. It only reached number seven, for goodness' sake! Some people would love a flop that only got to number seven. Arguably, it's not one of the stronger songs. If you listen to it on the Gold album, some would say that it's just filler, but there are a lot of artists that would love filler of that quality. I think that it deserves a place on the album because it's part of the ABBA story. As a single it was a little bit less vibrant, and the chorus doesn't seem to kick in like the other tracks. It's certainly not as powerful as, say, 'Dancing Queen'. Maybe they needed to put out a single for commercial reasons, and it did the job. It's not one of the greatest, but great nevertheless. The song was obviously geared for the disco market, with the damped guitar riffs and the plodding fours; you did have the big production chorus, but it generally wasn't as effervescent as other ABBA singles.

The use of melancholy lyrics became very important to ABBA in their later years. 'Lay All Your Love On Me' is patently about a woman's insecurities about her relationship, about her worries that her man's going to stray. Everyone in the world can relate to those lyrics. So many people had been in those same situations, and yet here was our favourite group, ABBA, renowned for uplifting choruses, singing about the darker side of relationships.

You've got the euphoria of things like 'Take a Chance on Me' and 'Dancing Queen' alongside 'Lay All Your Love on Me' and 'The Name of The Game', which have quite dark lyrics, yet those two types of songs could co-exist perfectly in the ABBA repertoire. We were more than happy to get a depressing lyric from them, because the overall production and the way that it was crafted was just immensely appealing, however you look at it.

RL: 'One of Us' is a great song, and it's an interesting sort of take, the rhythm. It's kind of a white man's reggae, if I can say that. I think I read something that they asked the bass player to just come up with whatever was going through his head – listen to the song a few times and chuck in a bass line that would go with it – and Rutger Gunnarsson is one of the best players in the world, I'd say. I think he just married the whole thing together; it was just perfect. That's probably one of the reasons why I think it's one of their best songs. I think that the reggae feel works so well for that song.

HF: By the time we get to 'One Of Us', the boys in ABBA were getting nervous about asking the girls to redo a vocal part for fear that it might provoke an argument or a row, and were taking the easy option, which wasn't necessarily the right option in terms of the song. Even the beat seems to be struggling; at one point ABBA could make that pompous German beat sound really sprightly. Now it was just starting to drag, and it was starting to sound laboured. Again, what had come naturally was no longer doing so, and was having to be forced – and, of course, by now the implications of their break-up, collectively and as two couples, was being felt.

RL: I found it amazing that they were having hit songs that were about the break-down of their relationships. 'One of Us' is a great example there. I suppose that's where good writing often comes from: personal experience. I think that they portrayed it really well.

HF: 'The Day Before You Came' is built on banks of electronic instruments that provide a strong atmosphere for Frida's vocals, but her vocals are mixed into the distance and they give it a rather kind of cold, objective feeling, almost as if she's looking down on the rest of us – in fact, looking down on the rest of ABBA, I suspect.

The song has a theatrical element in the sense that by now Björn and Benny were thinking of stage productions when writing their music. I think that they already knew this was going to be the next stage, after ABBA had finished, and I think by now they could see that the end was in sight, and they were already looking beyond to what was going to come next. They were interested in live performances, perhaps something that they had never really been able to fulfil properly with ABBA, maybe owing to the fact that they were not the world's finest stage performers. They were perhaps a little too self-conscious on stage with ABBA to make it work, but I think that Björn and Benny were increasingly interested in writing music to be performed live…

RL: I think that they had their sights set on writing musicals. They moved pretty quickly on to writing Chess [a 1984 musical that Benny and Björn wrote with lyricist Tim Rice] and similar kinds of things not long after ABBA ceased to record any more. I don't think they actually split up, allegedly. 'When All is Said and Done' I think is a great song, because it looks at the positive side of a divorce, of what's left after the wash-up, so I see it as being a positive song. I think that there was some noteworthiness in what they were doing in those last albums, and I think those songs are quite valid. Certainly, 'One of Us' became a huge hit in many countries around the world.

HF: By the Visitors album, ABBA were no longer two couples, they were two songwriters who had developed a telepathic understanding of what worked, and two distinctive voices who no longer blended quite as well as they had done in the past. Björn and Benny were also writing music that had ambitions beyond their usual formula. They were experimenting with different kinds of sounds, probably because they were looking beyond ABBA to what they would be writing next.

Some of the melodies on Visitors have an almost operatic quality, which certainly made the girls work harder and brought something new out in them. They could sing for themselves now, while Björn and Benny looked at other ways of writing songs and what else they could bring to their own song writing. What the album doesn't have is that vivacious dance element which had been such a cornerstone of earlier ABBA records. Those songs will last forever. People will be playing ABBA songs in 100 years time; there's no question of that, but with this album they had effectively run themselves dry.

'Under Attack' is from the last Abba recording session, in August 1982. It's an interesting experiment in a lush, synthesised pop-music style, one that's actually a bit reminiscent of Buggles in the way that they use synthesisers and harmonies together. You can hear elements of this style in the Police's album Synchronicity, which would go on to be a mammoth album, particularly in America. There's no doubt that, by now, ABBA were influencing all sorts of bands around them. Not just other pop bands, who were doing mediocre versions of ABBA songs, a trend that has continued to this day, but rock bands as well were taking many of the ideas that ABBA had pioneered and were now incorporating them into rock music. That gave another dimension to ABBA's music, one that ABBA themselves couldn't follow up, but other bands could.

PW: 'Thank You for the Music' was originally released in 1978 on the B-side of 'Eagle', and it wasn't until 1983 that it was released as a single in the UK, eventually reaching number 33. Having said that, it encapsulates what ABBA were all about, and the public's feelings towards them. It first appeared on The Album; on the second side of that record there was a mini-musical called The Girl With the Golden Hair. This was the song that the girl sang about being a bit of a dumbo, but being very good at music. I tend to think that it was as a thank you for the fans. There was a cover of it that Steps did later on [in fact a medley entitled Thank ABBA for the Music, released in 1999] that showed how much the world loved ABBA. They were the kind of phenomenon that may never come along again, and 'Thank You for the Music' really just sums it all up for me.

HF: It features a compelling Agnetha vocal, capturing one of her strongest performances. It's a pretty cheesy song, but of course ABBA can get away with that; they knew exactly how to get away with that by now. Other bands would make it sound a lot cheesier, and it probably wouldn't have been a hit. It is, of course, now better known as the inevitable climax to every ABBA tribute band show.

PW: It's timeless, but still very old fashioned, rather like something from a Broadway show, with its tongue firmly in its cheek. The only thing that's missing is a, "Thank you very much and goodnight", right at the end.

RL: Yes, 'Thank You for the Music' is seen to be the end of the ABBA era. I guess it's a retrospective, and yes, we often use it for our final song, to finish a concert, and it's kind of appropriate for that. I think it works in many ways, starting off with just a piano and a voice, it's a ballad, and then the choruses pick up, it's uplifting. It's a great song.

After our discussion, we cornered Leissle and asked him to reflect on his

personal reaction to ABBA's music, and the way in which it has affected his career.

Q You said earlier that you were too embarrassed to go and see ABBA when they sang in Melbourne…
RL: When I was a teenager, I had to pretend that I liked English progressive rock music within my peer group. I couldn't really admit that I liked any ABBA songs, although I did, and actually a lot of us did!

Q Are lot of people frightened that it is uncool to like ABBA?
RL: Well, when ABBA started playing disco songs, I guess I could hear them on TV and hear them on the radio and stuff and I could appreciate it. I must admit that I sat there on my bed with my guitar trying to figure out what they were playing. I guess I warmed to ABBA a bit more in that period.

Q Do you think they are/were a cool band or a slightly uncool band?
RL: I think ABBA were both a cool and an uncool band. I think that there was a period when I was a teenager when you couldn't admit that you had heard an ABBA song on the radio, and that you'd quite liked it. On the other hand, I think that they were cool in that they stuck to their guns, and they did what they did in their own way. I think that is one of the many reasons why people can appreciate ABBA's music today, simply because they are great songs, incredibly well performed and produced. Some of the stuff that they did straddles the cool and the uncool, like some of the clothes that they wore! Some were just beyond belief, but some were great, you know.

Q I don't understand why it was that people thought they were uncool. What is it about them that you weren't allowed to admit that you liked in them, and why?
RL: In that period, there was a lot of serious music around – punk was just beginning, and there were many different offshoots from punk. I suppose that ABBA lacked the guitar thing in a lot of the songs, although some of their tracks did have some edgier guitar stuff. I think that ABBA were seen as a pop band, but – definitely when they were trying to break America – they tried to turn the ship a bit and turn into more of a rock band so that they could be appreciated by the American audience, and it was somewhat unsuccessful. I think that they will go down in history as being one of the best pure pop bands that there ever has been.

Q Did ABBA go through different stages of their career when their influences were different?

RL: I think that certainly, ABBA had different periods. To begin with, they were trying to win over the Eurovision audience, and they really focused on how to write the perfect pop song. I think that they followed what they saw as being musical trends throughout the rest of their career. They went through a whole disco phase, writing songs that they thought would be appreciated by people who were into disco music. They wrote some classic power ballads as well. 'Winner Takes It All' is a great example of them writing an incredibly moving ballad.

Q What do you think were their career highlights?

RL: Having a succession of incredible top-10 and number-one pop hits has to be a highlight, and also having the ability to write such an amazing string of songs that went nowhere near the charts. I think that they had something like 20 or 30 songs which were excellent pieces of work but were just album tracks and – for me personally, I go back and rediscover some of those songs and really enjoy them, I must say.

Q What kind of audience do you get at your shows?

RL: ABBA have such a wide appeal, they really do. Nowadays we're seeing kids at Björn Again concerts who've obviously heard Madonna sampling 'Gimme, Gimme, Gimme', and they want to see that kind of music being played live; so we're seeing that kind of differentiation in ages, certainly, at Björn Again shows. We get older people as well, people in their 70s come down to have a bit of a bop at our gigs. People can remember ABBA from the 70s and want to have a bit of a nostalgia trip and hear it all again. That's why the musical Mamma Mia is so popular and remains so, eight years after it was first put on. Still, I should think that there may be certain parts in the deep South of England where there are people who are into heavy metal music and would claim that they had never even listened to an ABBA track. That would be sinful.

Q Do you know what the band think of Björn Again? Do they approve of the way in which their legacy is dealt with? Just why is it so popular – why is it such a big industry?

RL: Well ABBA are fully aware of Björn Again. We met up with Benny and Björn in Stockholm in '92 – we'd been touring around for a few years and we were touring Sweden – and someone in the record company mentioned to Benny and Björn that we were around, you know – should they want to get us into the studio, and beat us up or something. Well, I don't know what their plan was, but they actually invited us into the studio and wanted to hear about what we were doing.

So we went in and had a chat to them and it was great. It was really quite productive, and they were fascinated to see that we were touring around the world, you know, wearing their costumes and playing their songs. I think they liked that, rather than being a direct copy of what ABBA did, we were trying to put our own slant on the whole thing. They found it quite interesting that we were a bit of a parody on them; which, to me, was natural. I mean what else would you do? I think that they quite appreciated that, and they had a really good sense of humour. Moreover, they were fascinated to hear that people were coming to our concerts, you know, because they honestly thought that their music was dead and buried – the whole ABBA thing, the fashion of the 70s, was finished in the late 80s and early 90s. I think that they took this on board, and they had had discussions about releasing a compilation CD, which became ABBA Gold, but they had no idea how popular that would be. We indicated to them that we thought it would be a great idea because our shows were going well – so, naturally, it follows. So, they released it and we know it went down really well, sold really well, and in fact is still doing so today.

Q Do you think that's where they got the whole idea for Mamma Mia from?
RL: It's a bit hard to say, but I'd like to think that we had something to do with it. I think that's a culmination of various things. I do know that we were behind the inspiration for P. J. Hogan writing Muriel's Wedding, because he was a Björn Again fan. Indeed, Erasure were fans of Björn Again, but also, you know, obviously fans of ABBA, so that was one of the reasons behind them coming out with a number-one [The EP, Abba-esque] which comprised four ABBA covers [Björn Again responded with their own EP, Erasure-ish]. So there are a number of factors associated with ABBA and Mamma Mia and Björn Again, but I think that we were certainly a catalyst.

Q Is it tricky for you to re-create that ABBA sound on stage?
RL: With Björn Again we've got some wonderful machines. We can have a

computer on stage which we can record backing vocals on, and there are things like percussion and so forth tend to – we normally go with a six-piece band, but the output is musically similar to the 12-piece band that ABBA would have toured. For us, the economics are much better going with a six-piece band. That means that we can afford to do it!

Q I was going to ask you about the parody element of your show, because you mentioned that your aim was always to put your own slant on performing ABBA stuff. I remember that the Erasure video was very jokey as well. What's the idea? Why do you use parody, and why do ABBA lend themselves to parody so well?

RL: Well I think it would be a little bit kind of naff if we were trying to be, let's say a true tribute to ABBA and try to almost be ABBA on stage. I think that we definitely shy away from that, because, for a start, I don't think it can really be done. You can try but I don't think you'd succeed; it wouldn't be a great formula. I think there's an inherent humorous quality to dressing up in ABBA costumes for a start, you know. It's not normal activity, really, or normal behaviour, so it's an in-built kind of parody.

Also, when we're on stage, when we're in the costumes and in character, we put on Swenglish accents – which are half Swedish, half English – because we all know that they had a funny kind of lingo. It was quite humorous, and in a way it was quite sweet, but their grasp of the English language and their grammar was as bad as mine just now. No, I mean, their grasp of the English language was a bit strange, so we play it up. On stage, we'll emulate Frida and Benny being a couple – Benny courting Frida, and Frida repulsing his advances – with Björn and Agnetha being more in love on stage, and stuff like that. I think that's what works very well for us, and kind of sets us apart. I think it's also the thing that Benny and Björn recognised and appreciated. They could understand where we were coming from, and they liked the sense of humour. That parody was played out in Erasure's video clip as well.

Q Is the visual element very important then?

RL: The visual image was a big part of ABBA's success. Their manager, Stig Anderson, was able to stand back and have a good look at the band. He fundamentally understood what the band needed, initially to win Eurovision, and then to go on beyond that. They have such a fantastic iconic look about them. You've got a dark-haired girl, a blonde-haired girl, a guy with a beard, a guy without a beard, and they all were represented as being as a similar kind height. If you look at their video clips they're all sort of even, and so there was a g deal of symmetry about the band as well, and I think that was probably capped with the logo, when the first 'B' in 'ABBA' was reversed [in 1976]. So symmetrical was, you know, two and two makes four.

Q How important were stage costumes to ABBA's image?

RL: ABBA's costumes were very important to their live image. They had to try present themselves in a fresh new way, as they did in the 70s, and look differen other bands. They had some great costumes – kimonos, costumes with brig coloured cats on them, which were quite exciting. I remember one film clip wh they had long versions of these cat costumes, which they tore off in a Bucks Fizz s during one of the songs, which was great!

Q Why did they use costumes? I mean, what did it do for us? What did it do them? Can you imagine them without those costumes, I suppose?

RL: It's hard to say. I suppose that, initially, they were trying to win the Eurovi song contest, and they knew that they had to look at more than just the music. T had to present themselves in such a way that they'd stand out. The costumes for AI

Abba live in concert, with Benny and Bjorn on the guitars and Anni-Frid and Agnetha leading the vocals

were very important, and, as we see nowadays, very iconic. Everyone remembers the costumes that ABBA were wearing, especially when they turned around and you saw 'Benny', 'Björn', 'Agnetha' and 'Frida' written on their backs.

Q Did they drop the crazy outfits as time went on? Was that part of fashion moving on or was that part of ABBA maturing do you think? Does it make any difference to the shows?

RL: I think that once ABBA had established themselves as superstars in the 70s, they wanted to get away from wearing those kind of costumes, the silly costumes, so they went for a more kind of an 80s look, I would say, wearing suits and stuff like that. The girls' clothes were very played down. I think that they were trying to show that they'd moved on quite a bit as a band, and musically as well.

Q Were ABBA content just to reproduce their recorded sound on their TV appearances?

RL: I think that when you saw the ABBA film clips they certainly wanted to keep their studio production. You very rarely saw them playing something live, unless it was Abba: The Movie, or some of the TV shows from America and Japan. I think, because it was so hard to reproduce their sound, they had a lot of their stuff on backing tracks, and they preferred to show themselves on television in that light.

Q Did they like the television format?

RL: Thanks to Queen, with the 'Bohemian Rhapsody' clip being such a major success, I think that ABBA realised that television was the best medium to use to sell the band, especially in the markets where they hadn't had much success, like Japan and America.

Q Did they seem comfortable on television, or do you think they were always worried about getting it right?

RL: I think that ABBA evolved over the years to be good at presenting themselves on TV. I mean, the film clips are great fun, but then, when they realised they had to show themselves as being a live band, which was very important back in the 70s and 80s, I think they paid too much attention to how they were perceived on television and so brought in their studio engineers to work in the television studio to recreate that sound, and also their vision people I suppose, to make sure they looked right.

Q Okay, why didn't they achieve the same level of success in America as they did everywhere else around the world?

RL: ABBA didn't have the same degree of success in America as they did in the rest of the world, certainly in Europe, partly due to the fact that they weren't really pigeon-holed in America. They weren't a Country band. They weren't a Rock band. They were something else. They were Euro-Pop, which the Americans didn't really understand. They did have a measure of success, but nowhere near as much as they did in Europe, of course. They tried a few new songs; 'Hey, Hey, Helen' would be one song in particular which had more of a guitar edge to it, and they played that on American TV, perhaps so that the Americans would see them as a rock outfit! 'On and On and On' is another one. But of course when their disco era came in, with songs like 'Gimme, Gimme, Gimme', 'Voulez-Vous', and 'Summer Night City', they really made their mark in America. Of course, 'Dancing Queen' would be their crowning glory.

Q Do you think any of it is down to touring? They didn't tour very much did they?

RL: They did some touring in America, but nowhere near enough really. For any band, especially in the US, once you put an album out, you need to tour to support it, really, but their philosophy was, 'Let's get on television, let's get on the biggest programmes we can' – The Dick Cavett Show, and those kind of programmes – that's how they wanted to present themselves to the wider American market.

Q How much of their style was simply studio creation? With something like 'Dum, Dum, Diddle', how did they manage to make such a ludicrous and quite banal song come alive?

RL: I think ABBA had that special quality about them. They could put ridiculous lyrics into a song, and because they were fundamentally great songwriters, they could make it work. A line like "Dum, dum, diddle, to be your fiddle" doesn't really make a great deal of sense, but it still works because I think it's something you can sing along to and enjoy.

Q It's funny isn't it? Because would we accept that from any other band? How is it that ABBA got away with it?

RL: ABBA could get away with it, I think, because they had that great image. The two girls – well, I think that every guy, and I think most women, could appreciate the two girls in the band – and the guys were cute as well. They had an appealing image that everyone could relate to in some way, so in theory they could put out any sort of rubbish and get away with it, but the fact of the matter is they did loads and loads of fantastic songs, even if a few weren't quite so great.

Q Top three songs?
RL: My three favourite ABBA songs would be 'The Winner Takes it All', it's a great song; 'Gimme, Gimme, Gimme (a Man After Midnight)', not so much for the lyrical content, but I think it's a really powerful song, and 'Knowing Me Knowing You'.

Q Why 'Knowing Me Knowing You'?
RL: I think 'Knowing Me Knowing You' is a great song. For a start I can play it on the guitar. It's a great pop song with a bit of a rocky edge to it. There's a great solo in there which is quite melodic. The guitar solo sits there really well, and just when you want it get massive, the guitar solo splits off and goes into this harmonic guitar break, which is kind of a bit of a rock thing, so there are very rocky guitar bits in there, and again, they used a kind of electric piano, I think, with a phased loop, and then they would break into acoustic piano. There's some great stuff in there. Musically, it's a great song.

Hugh Fielder also had some things to add when we spoke to him after our group discussion.

Q How do you think ABBA fit into popular music history?
HF: The comparison is often made between the Beatles and ABBA, and in sound terms there's quite a lot to be said for the fact that ABBA took the Beatles' ideas and ran with them. However, there's a funny thing about British rock music, and the way that the Europeans translate it. They somehow seem to get the style, but they don't always get the substance. With ABBA, that didn't really matter, because the style was just so superb that you weren't, by the end, listening to the substance. I mean, are you going to start listening to the words of 'Mamma Mia' and work out what they're all about? I don't think so.

Q You said before that ABBA were not really a presence on the live circuit at the time, so were people aware of what they looked like if they were so –

I don't mean they were reclusive but…

HF: Oh yes, people were certainly aware of what they looked like, because it wasn't just about the music, it was about the fashion, and nobody perpetrated more crimes against the fashion industry than ABBA did in their day. I mean, some of them were pretty atrocious, but then we are talking about the 70s, and it was the time that fashion forgot. Even though the gypsy skirts may be coming back now, I've got a feeling that hot pants really won't – certainly not those wild bell-bottom trousers they used to wear, with the sort of skin-tight legs down to the knee that flowed out to, goodness knows how many inches at the bottom – and that was just the boys. You should see some of the girls' outfits. By now, people were getting quite interested in ABBA – intrigued maybe. The idea of two couples was an interesting one; people wanted to know more about it and were looking at the songs to see what they might give away. In fact, they weren't giving much away at this point. Björn and Benny were certainly workaholics by now, and absolutely obsessed with their craft and what they were doing, but you got the feeling that the girls would quite like a life. They'll do their part, and they'll do it very well, but their outlook was slightly broader. Björn and Benny were definitely looking inwards a lot, and that shows in the relationship between the arrangements and the voices.

Q What were their musical hallmarks, would you say?

HF: A typical ABBA song consisted of a strong beat, a contagious melody, intense backing instruments – usually keyboards with perhaps acoustic guitars, layered very thickly – with the voices added on top, which was the special ABBA ingredient. It was the multi-layered approach which was very much a characteristic in the 70s. When it got to the 80s they tended to use a slightly sparser sound, using many more electronic instruments, like synthesisers and drum machines.

The production and mixing process in an ABBA song were crucial in creating the ABBA magic. It's no coincidence that the regular studio engineer at their studios was a Phil Spector fan, and that's the reason that the instruments tended to get doubled up. Instead of using one acoustic guitar, he'd double up and use two, possibly four. Same thing with pianos and other instruments that came in. It created a lush sound and was actually warmer than the Phil Spector wall of sound, but at the same time more fluid than the punchy Motown pop sound that they were also fascinated by.

Q Had they always been that polished then?

HF: Yeah, I think right from the beginning. Björn and Benny's arrangements are a genial mix of craftsmanship and intuition. The craftsmanship was in knowing how to create an effect, at any point during the song, that would highlight exactly what the song was trying to achieve, and the intuition came from knowing exactly where to put it, and where not to put it. With music, like with so many other things, it's what you leave out that becomes important. It enables you to increase the range of dynamics. With a simple line that is repeated twice, all you've got to do is change something subtly in the backing and the second repetition takes on a completely different flavour.

Q Has anybody written songs like them since, do you think?

HF: No, I don't think anybody has written like ABBA since, mainly because there's no need to, since ABBA did it so well. What else would you want to do with it, apart from simply repeat it? That's why people go to see Mamma Mia; it's why they queue up to see Björn Again. They don't necessarily want something new from that style; they just want the originals. They were perfect. You couldn't really improve on them – just hear them again really.

Q What do you think were their career highlights?

HF: ABBA's musical highlights were their singles, really, which is why they sold far more singles than they ever did albums. In fact, the one album that anyone runs out to buy is ABBA Gold, which consists of all their singles. Enough said, really.

Q Why do you think that they were, well are, so enduringly successful? What is it about them?

HF: ABBA made pop music that is, in a sense, timeless. It typifies its era in many ways, and it transcends that era. It's cosy and it's nostalgic. Even if you weren't born when ABBA were having their biggest hits, when you listen to them you feel a sense of comfort, nostalgia, cosiness – it's homely and it's everything good pop music should be. It's not trying to be anything it isn't. It's not trying to pioneer a new style. It's not trying to promote the individual personalities. There's nothing about ABBA that pretends to be better than they actually were. At their best, ABBA were just as good as their songs, and their songs were absolutely brilliant. That's perhaps why they have lasted so long and will continue to last.

I don't think ABBA were retro at the time. At the time when ABBA were most popular, pop music was perhaps not at the height of fashion. It was certainly not at the height of fashion among people who were listening to rock music. Rock music was diversifying into a million different styles. There were bands of exceptional musical ability. There were bands pioneering progressive rock, blues rock, heavy metal – all kinds of styles were breaking through in the 70s. ABBA, in a sense, were clinging on to the old pop music values, and those values were pretty unfashionable among most people who followed rock music at that time. On their own terms, ABBA made very progressive pop music, and that's perhaps why they continue to have such an appeal now – because the music they made was better than the other pop music being made at the time, and the best will always survive.

But ABBA were not just about the music; it was just part of the whole package. They had pop promos, they had their costumes, even if some of the costumes had a lot to answer for. The whole thing of having two couples added immediate intrigue, while you worked out who was actually with who, and how that worked together. You couldn't really tell, because they didn't make it obvious. It added to the intrigue; it gave them identity, and on top of that the music provided the cream, because the music was the outstanding part of the package.

Q Do you think ABBA were and are cool?

HF: No, I don't think that ABBA were ever cool. I remember working on a music paper at the time of ABBA's biggest hits, and we would ring up the record company and ask them to send over ABBA albums under a fictitious name so that nobody else knew that they were ours. I think that probably continues to this day!

Q Why do you think that is?

HF: People who don't like ABBA will generally admit to liking more progressive, more sophisticated musical styles. ABBA don't represent anything terribly sophisticated in terms of style. They are incredibly sophisticated in terms of technique, but pop has never been cool, and probably never will be. It's something that you're supposed to grow into, and then grow out of – perhaps move on to something more serious – real music, maybe. ABBA proved that that isn't so. There is good pop music that works for its own sake and is there on its own terms. It's a fine line – there's a fine line between, say, ABBA songs, or Brotherhood of Man, or Blue Mink, or even 'Agadoo', but ABBA managed to

ABBA at the pinnacle of their career

walk that line. They knew the difference, and they never let their standards slip.

Q Do you think it's because they're European and not British?

HF: It's not that they weren't British; they were Swedish more than they were European, really. Their take on pop music was so sophisticated; it was erudite, and yet it knew that it was just pop music, and so they made the best of a style that was not groundbreaking. It was popular music. It was meant to be liked, and it was meant to be bought in large quantities. Too much of the European take on British rock music has tended to exist in terms of style rather than substance. ABBA managed to get to the substance of pop music, and indeed the style as well, even though the style was a very transitional, short-lived affair, as pop music should be. Pop music is here today, gone tomorrow, because there will always be another pop song. ABBA didn't think that their pop songs would last for as long as they have. That's because they were excellent craftsman.

Q So, then, are they pop?

HF: Yes they are. ABBA are perfect pop. There's nothing else. there's nothing you can read into ABBA songs. Trying would be like trying to read something into soap operas. ABBA are pop in the same way that soap operas are pop; you don't try and compare a soap opera to a Shakespearean drama. In the same way, you don't try and turn ABBA into the Rolling Stones. They simply took the pop style and perfected it to such an extent that nobody has been able to match them since.

By 1982, ABBA were in serious trouble. Both couples had divorced (Björn and Agnetha had split in 1980, soon to be followed by Benny and Frida the following year), and although their relationship difficulties had been the basis for some of their most powerful songs, the group's records were starting to sound jaded and bitter.

The group's individual members were already beginning to pursue other activities – Björn and Benny with their musical, Chess, and Agnetha with her successful solo career in Sweden – and so it was Frida's turn for a high profile solo project, on this occasion an album prophetically entitled Something's Going On.

Enlisting the illustrious and tremendously talented Phil Collins, Frida and the Genesis singer/drummer brought in a collection of world-class musician buddies and chose songs running the gamut from Bryan Ferry and Rod Argent to Russ Ballard and Giorgio Moroder. The title track, penned by English singer/songwriter Ballard, climbed to number 13 in the U.S. and remained there for a dozen weeks.

In this contemporary interview, Frida presented herself as a gracious and ingratiating singer who had been willing to take a deep plunge into unknown waters. In a classy hotel located in New York's expensive section, she spoke about her record, her work with ABBA, and, underneath it all, tried to express the feelings of searching for an identity, for all her remarkable wealth and accomplishments, that she felt she was still somehow missing.

Q Though this is certainly the most successful and highly publicized solo record you've ever made, it's really nothing new for you to step away from ABBA.
Anni-Frid Lyngstad: In a sense it is, because it was a long time ago that I made a solo album, and I have been with ABBA for 12 years.
Q Did you feel a certain sense of creative urgency? Did you feel that you had to make an album that was as musically engaging as your work with ABBA?

Frida: When I made the attempt to do something on my own, of course I knew that people probably would compare what I was doing with ABBA, but that didn't bother me at all. I wanted to do something that I felt strongly about.

Q You are not a songwriter yourself?

Frida: No, I am not, but I would like to try. I will sit down and see if there's something there.

Q So meeting a songwriter like Phil Collins must have been an amazing experience?

Frida: Do you know this? It's a cute little story. My daughter had a cassette, and on the cassette was 'In The Air Tonight'. I thought it was an excellent song, although I didn't know about Phil at that time. She told me who he was, and I got the album and listened to it over and over again. When I decided to do an album of my own, I wanted him to produce it.

Q Phil was your first choice as producer?

Frida: Yes, he was, and my only one. If he had said no, I don't think I would have done the album.

Q Did you know about Phil's earlier work with Genesis?

Frida: Yes, I knew about Genesis, but I didn't know about Phil.

Q And how did you come to use Hugh Padgham as an engineer?

Frida: I mean, he has been the engineer for Phil for quite a long time, I think, and Phil wanted to have him.

Q Are you happy with the actual sound quality of the album?

Frida: Yes, very much, I am.

Q Did Hugh actually make suggestions about different types of microphones and how to record your voice?

Frida: Yeah. We tried different mikes, and I noticed that in these rock and roll types of songs, or the pop songs, if I used a Shure mike – I think that's what it was – it worked really good. For example, 'Tell Me It's Over' and songs like that.

Q You recorded the album at ABBA's Polar Studios; do you know what type of recording gear was used?

Frida: We did everything at our studio except the strings and horns, which we recorded at AIR Studios in London. I know we recorded it digital but I'm not very much into that technical thing.

Q ABBA is obviously a group very concerned with the sound of the records they make.
Frida: Yes, they are, but I think this, compared to ABBA, is a little bit different. Engineers all work in different ways, treat the facilities differently. Hugh is very competent, very talented, and I think he knew what he wanted out of us and how to treat us.

Q How aware are the buyers of this album that you are a member of Abba? Do they know who you are?
Frida: I don't think so; not in the U.S. and not even in Europe. I don't think people connect me with the group, if they recognize me at all. I don't know. Because in a way I've changed. Before I had long hair, and then I cut it off…

Q Your record seems a natural move away from ABBA and not a project that was going to use the band as a stepping stone. Is this what you were trying to achieve?
Frida: Yeah, maybe. I wanted it to be something separate from ABBA, for it to be considered apart from the fact that I am a member of the group. I want it to be very personal, very much Frida.

Q You chose songs to reveal a different side of your musical personality?
Frida: I chose the songs from my heart. I really wanted to feel very strongly for every individual song. I wanted to feel great emotion for the songs.

Q What has been the reaction, thus far, from fans of ABBA who have heard the album?
Frida: Very positive. I got a lot of fan mail telling me how much they like it.

Q Have you given any thought about going out on your own to do a solo tour?
Frida: Not yet, I would like to wait. I think it's too early; I will know when the time is right. I would also like to record another album before doing it. I mean, I would like to have more than 11 songs to take out on the road!

Q So, ideally, this may turn into an ongoing venture – for you to make solo records and potentially promote the music on the road?
Frida: Yes, I would like it to go on, if it doesn't interfere with my work with ABBA.

Q Have your band mates heard the album?
Frida: They like it very much – so they tell me! I hope they're honest.

Q How did you come to choose 'I Know There's Something Going On' as

the single? It's a brilliant song but it's also the longest track on the album.

Frida: I wanted it to be a single. I knew it when I heard it. It is the longest song on the album, but we edited the song for a single version so it's shorter. It's four minutes, 24 seconds; I thought that was short enough.

Q: Did you listen to more contemporary types of singers in order to hear what other female vocalists were doing? People like Stevie Nicks, Pat Benatar, or Debby Harry from Blondie?

Frida: I listened to a lot of Pat Benatar, because I didn't know of her either. It was my daughter, as well. She has been very good for me. She has gotten me interested in Pat Benatar because she thought she was a very, very good singer – the way she arranges the songs and the way she uses the songs and everything. I like the sound of it very much.

Q The single does have some of those Benatar-type guitar/vocal arrangements in it.

Frida: I asked her if she was interested in writing a song for me, but she didn't have the time. Oh, I don't know – maybe she didn't want to!

Q But Pat certainly knew about you and your work with ABBA...

Frida: I think so. I mean, I didn't make personal contact with her. I don't know if she knew who I was!

Q How did you find the various musicians who appear on the record?

Frida: That was Phil. I mean, I wanted to move away from the Swedish music scene, so I wanted him to choose the musicians. I've been working with Swedish people for so long, so I wanted to try something different.

[Collins brought in members from Earth, Wind & Fire to augment his menagerie of gifted players that included Mo Foster, Daryl Stuermer, and Peter Robinson.]

Q How was it different working with English musicians, as opposed to Swedish players?

Frida: Swedish musicians are very good, skilled people, but I saw it as a challenge. In a way, I worked differently on this album than I did with ABBA; I was in the studio all the time, singing along with the musicians while they were rehearsing the songs. Actually, we became more like a band than studio musicians working together with a solo artist. It was a very nice feeling. With ABBA, all the music is put down and I'm not even there. Then we come in and do all the vocals.

Q The songs on this record were a bit more up-tempo, and have more edge than most of the ABBA material. Did you deliberately sing in a different style, to find different places in your voice?

Frida: Yes, I did. In many ways I had to stretch my voice. That was a challenge. First of all I picked the songs that I liked – if they were rock and roll songs or ballads or whatever it was. I didn't think, 'Can I do this?' If you feel very strongly about something you can do it; you can stretch yourself.

Q Did you involve yourself in the final mix of a song to make sure everything sounded the way you wanted it to?

Frida: Yeah, I was very keen on the result. I listened very carefully to them, and if there was something I didn't like I immediately told Hugh and Phil about it.

Q Ultimately, did you have the final word on vocal presentation?

Frida: We had a very good communication, Phil and me, and if he didn't like something, he told me, and if I didn't like something, I told him. If I was satisfied, I told him also, and he respected very much what I said and what I thought.

Q Please don't shoot the journalist for saying this, but the ABBA records lack a certain warmth, a certain bonding of musician and singer that you've managed to achieve on your album. You mentioned earlier that typically all the music for an ABBA album was recorded, and then you and the other members would come in after the fact to lay down vocals.

Frida: Yeah, I know what you mean. Maybe we should do it the same way as I have been doing it here. Maybe the results would be different then; I think it's a very good idea and I think we should think it over. It's difficult, because after such a long time you get stuck in a kind of path. It's hard to step out from that within the band. I think I have reached what I wanted with doing this album. I think it's exactly the same thing that we should do within the group. Probably, we will gain something from my attempt. Agnetha will do a solo album at the beginning of next year, which Mike Chapman is producing, and hopefully she will work in the same way that I did. Then we can gain something in the group's work.

Q So, when you listen to your album, and the recent ABBA albums, can you hear a real change in your voice? Has it matured, do you think?

Frida: Oh, yes, of course it has changed. As you get older it changes, and you get very aware of how to use your voice in a technical way, because I'm working with it all the time.

Q Were you able to create final tracks in first and second takes? Or are you the type of singer who likes working on a song over and over to get that vocal just right?

Frida: I feel very comfortable in the studio, and it's usually a first or second take for most songs.

Q That's very impressive, especially since the songs on this album aren't exactly the easiest songs to sing.

Frida: Is it impressive? I think I'm a good singer. I don't like the idea of taking vocals from many different takes. I'd rather perform a song, maybe several times, and then maybe take the best out of every performance.

Q This is hard to imagine because you're in the studio or performing live almost constantly, but do you practice singing?

Frida: No, not nowadays, but I took singing lessons for many years and I know how to use my voice!

Just as Something's Going On was not Frida's first solo album, it was not her last, either, and although both girls have enjoyed solo successes, the most recent being Agnetha's My Colouring Book in 2004, nothing that they have done since has come close to matching the work that they did with ABBA. Nonetheless, ABBA is a continuing phenomenon, and the music that this humble quartet made will forever live on in the canon of popular music.

ABBA performing in concert

ABBA track by track

ABBA – love them or hate them it is doubtful there is a person in the western world who wouldn't have heard of ABBA. Hugely successful in the seventies ABBA were a band with dozens of songs with catchy hooks. These were songs that often raced up the charts as soon as they were released, in turn the single releases catapulted the albums to the top of the charts the world over making million for the band. Over four hundred millions sales worldwide in fact! The band were for a while the biggest export out of any Scandinavian country.

ABBA had so many hits, one might be forgiven for thinking that they were just a singles band. In fact they recorded eight fully fledged studio albums and their career also spawned a double live album and several exceptional videos and DVDs. Compilations are in another league altogether with releases like ABBA Gold still holding its own as one of the best selling releases of all time. Over twenty years after the band split they are as popular as ever and their music is being heard in ever increasing circles due in part to the immense success of the stage show Mama Mia.

In the seventies, ABBA were the most popular band in Australia. Today that fact has not changed; they are still the most popular band in the land of OZ as far as sales are concerned. Ever! The Best Of ABBA is still Australia's best selling album of all time. Some might question what that says about the record buying public in the land down-under.

Whatever one feels about the music of ABBA only a fool would deny the fact they were masters in the field of pop, both in composition and the ability to market their product. The music they generated in the seventies is amongst the most well known and influential from that decade. After all where would Madonna be without the groundwork and influence supplied by one of pop's greatest?

RING RING

Originally released 26th March 1973.
Sweden: Polar Music POLS242,
UK: Polydor 843 642-2
CD re-master, 2001:
Polar Music 549 950-2

Although not a groundbreaking album it is ABBA-esque enough for any fan to want to own this one. As the band's debut it does contain a number of clever songs although the highlight for most would almost certainly be the catchy Ring, Ring. Recording for the album took place in various Stockholm studios and lasted for over a year from March 1972 through

March 1973. Interestingly the album was pretty much a side project for entry into the Eurovision Song contest put together by Stig Anderson, Benny and Björn and using the girls almost as session musicians. The album in fact was originally released under their full Christian names and only later was it shortened to ABBA. Clever stuff all in all.

RING RING *(B Andersson / S Anderson / B Ulvaeus / N Sedaka / P Cody)*

This track probably more than any other on the album signifies the sound ABBA would make their signature sound. Although the tracks certainly improved over the years following Ring, Ring this tune really does carry the characteristics that were to catapult ABBA to international stardom. The writing team of Benny and Björn were writing prospective hits even at this early stage of ABBA's career.

Stig Anderson also drafted in Neil Sedaka and his writing partner Phil Cody to supply lyrics that would be acceptable to an English ear. This they did, although one can certainly debate the quality of the lyric! What one cannot question is the catchiness of this pop song. Listen to this and it will be resonating in your head for a long time afterwards and that was certainly one of the secrets of ABBA's success.

ANOTHER TOWN, ANOTHER TRAIN *(B Andersson / B Ulvaeus)*

Fairly mediocre track that did eventually end up on the Greatest Hits collection. Not sure why as it was never a hit! Lead vocal by Björn. Gentle and rather pleasant piano and other keyboard toys by Benny. The best part of the track is almost certainly the chorus where the girls do their thing. Album filler at best.

DISILLUSION *(A Fältskog / B Ulvaeus)*

Interesting for the fact this is the only Agnetha song to ever be recorded and included on an ABBA album! What is surprising is that she had already proven she could write catchy numbers during her preceding solo career. It certainly has a typical heartrending vocal from her in this one and was a sign of things to come.

PEOPLE NEED LOVE *(B Andersson / B Ulvaeus)*

Gary Puckett and the Union Gap would have had a field day with this little ditty! Nice try but it doesn't really go anywhere. Interestingly it was the band's very first single (recorded in early 1972) and was inspired by English hit group Blue Mink although it was certainly not up to the standard of the material Blue Mink was generating at the time. First single it may have been, a hit it was not.

I SAW IT IN THE MIRROR (B Andersson / B Ulvaeus)

A crap song with crap vocals! This one doesn't really seem to have a redeeming feature anywhere apart from the fact it used up two minutes, thirty four seconds of vinyl. Today in the age of ipod's it is one to program out. Forever!

NINA, PRETTY BALLERINA (B Andersson / B Ulvaeus)

Clever little start from a steam train (wonder which sound effect record that was lifted off). The track however is a catchy pop song that had this been recorded years later with better production may well have been a clever pop hit. Little did the band realise how prophetic the use of the cheering crowd would be for them.

LOVE ISN'T EASY (BUT IT SURE IS HARD ENOUGH)
(B Andersson / B Ulvaeus)

Another song that never quite seemed to get there. Quite possibly due to too much use of Benny and Björn's vocal. Released as a single in several Scandinavian countries (surprisingly not Sweden) it failed to chart anywhere. Not surprising really.

ME AND BOBBY AND BOBBY'S BROTHER (B Andersson / B Ulvaeus)

Another fairly typical early ditty that was not unlike 'Me and Bobby McGee' in melody at times. Nice playing but this was certainly nothing more than album filler.

HE IS YOUR BROTHER (B Andersson / B Ulvaeus)

The band's second single from the album, they were actually quite fond of this one. It was also a popular song in Australia and New Zealand and apart from the female vocal was quite similar to material that had been issued by New Zealand sixties pop group The Fourmyula. Quite possibly it was this similarity that gave it acceptance and fondness down-under.

SHE'S MY KIND OF GIRL *(B Andersson / B Ulvaeus)*

This could certainly have been issued in the sixties had ABBA been around as a group then – it also would have had a chance of being quite a big hit. It retains all the quaintness of the period. Not unlike material that Dutch group Golden Earrings had been pumping out with success in the mid sixties. Now here's the thing! It was in fact the very first single recorded by Benny and Björn in 1969 and released in 1970 to accompany a porn (soft one) movie called The Seduction Of Inga. It was re-released as the B-side of Ring, Ring and this was probably the reason for its eventual inclusion on an ABBA album despite the fact there is no contribution from the girls.

I AM JUST A GIRL *(B Andersson / S Anderson / B Ulvaeus)*

ABBA with trumpets and other horns – something they were to do way better in years to come however. Originally titled I Am Just A Man this had been recorded prior to the Ring Ring sessions for a children's movie by Jarl Kulle. Not one of ABBA's finest moments.

ROCK'N'ROLL BAND *(B Andersson / B Ulvaeus)*

One of the best bits of guitar playing ever heard on an ABBA album and worth it for that alone! Obviously rock and roll, it borrowed a lot from The Beatles through to Chuck Berry – all mixed in of course with that wonderful ABBA vocal sound. This one certainly had potential even if was originally a Björn and Benny single that had been re-jigged and female vocals added. It was however a nice little closer to the original album and it certainly showed the band had a sense of humour.

BONUS TRACKS:

MERRY-GO-ROUND *(B Andersson / B Ulvaeus)*

Originally recorded as a follow up single in Japan to She's My Kind Of Girl this was another Björn and Benny recording that had the girls' harmonies added. This album version was also released in Sweden as the B-side to People Need Love. Nice addition to have as a bonus track on the CD for all the completists and it's a nice bit of collector-ville for people who love the sounds of the sixties.

SANTA ROSA *(B Andersson / B Ulvaeus)*

Released as the B-side of He Is Your Brother in Sweden only. The song was another Björn and Benny number that had been dragged out of the vaults. This time however not originally for album inclusion but instead it was chosen by Epic their Japanese label for the band to perform at the Yamaha World Popular Song Contest. Agnetha and Frida accompanied them as backing singers although they do not contribute to the recording here. They didn't win the contest.

RING, RING (BARA DU SLOG EN SIGNAL)
(B Andersson / S Anderson / B Ulvaeus)

Swedish version of Ring, Ring this was to become their biggest success for 1972 and 1973 in their home country. The single topped the charts and actually stopped the English version of Ring, Ring single and album from reaching number one!

WATERLOO

Originally released 4th March 1974.
Sweden: Polar Music POLS252,
UK: Epic EPC 80179. CD re-master, 2001: Polar Music 549 951-2. Sound and Vision release, 2004: Polar 0602498664636 – features one audio disc and one separate DVD

The Ring, Ring album may not have been groundbreaking as an album however Waterloo certainly was as far as powerful pop was concerned. Recording for the album took place at Metronome Studios, Stockholm from late September 1973 through March 1974. It was during the recording sessions of the album that manager Stig Anderson once again got the band entered in the Eurovision song contest, a platform that he and the band believed could show the world that Swedes could deliver the goods as far as pop music was concerned. All he had to do was get the band up there on stage with a (soon to be) classic pop song and they would be able to prove it to the world.

Many a band and manager have thought this THE plan that could work. Unusually in this case Stig Anderson was right. ABBA won the song contest and quite frankly the rest is history. Waterloo the single was released all over the world (in several languages) and the follow up album sold by the truckload. ABBA had become a household name literally overnight and they were never to look back.

Although Waterloo (the album) does come across more as just a disparate collection of tracks rather than a cohesive album there are some very good tracks on the album. Indeed it is arguably more fun to listen to the album nowadays than it was in 1974.

WATERLOO (B Andersson / S Anderson / B Ulvaeus)

If any track were to signify the success and typify the sound then this one would surely be it! Not because it is a brilliant track or better than anything else they have ever done (it's not and they have certainly written better material). But it is a piece of its time and it was their first truly international hit. It is a clever catchy pop song and it was written as a piece to capture the hearts and minds of those judging the 1974 Eurovision song contest. This it did in no uncertain terms!

Once the band had been invited to contribute, work progressed quickly with Benny and Björn writing the music and Stig Anderson writing extremely catchy lyrics. Recording took place quickly and the band duly entered the contest.

Held in Brighton, England the TV world were subjected to the sight of two weirdly dressed male musicians, two extremely sexy female singers and a conductor dressed up as Napoleon. The band did not intend to come third (as in the previous year) or second. All they wanted was a first and that they got with resounding effect. Waterloo won in no uncertain terms and the song quickly became a hit all over the world. The success of the single ensured millions of sales for the album as well. ABBA had entered the big time and they hadn't done it by halves. The song itself is not unlike See My Baby Jive performed by The Wizzard – another song that had raced up the charts only a year earlier. The similarity would not be lost on many in the business.

SITTING IN THE PALMTREE (B Andersson / B Ulvaeus)

With a nice 'Island' feel, gentle lead vocal from Björn and wonderful backing vocals from the girls Sitting In The Palmtree still sounds good today. A catchy number this really is a timeless piece of pop.

KING KONG SONG (B Andersson / B Ulvaeus)
More of an 'American' pop song than the typical material ABBA was to generate. The song is catchy nonetheless and the keyboard sound will bring a smile to any musician's face. Only in the seventies!

HASTA MANANA (B Andersson / S Anderson / B Ulvaeus)
Until Tomorrow – this is one of the best tracks on the album and in fact one of the best pop songs ever recorded by ABBA. As a pop song it is pure genius and there is not a girl on the planet that wouldn't be wooed with this one in the right circumstances. Sure, the lyrics are a little trite but it's a good one all the same. The girls' vocals are superb and it became quite obvious to all concerned that with songs like this and two sexy women singing, ABBA were a force to be reckoned with. Featuring Agnetha as the lead singer the song was a perfect platform for stardom. Something they were to all enjoy for a long time.

Interestingly this was the original contender for the Eurovision entry, however at the last minute Stig Anderson and the band chose to break from the usual Euro formula (of which Hasta Mānana was a perfect contender) and go with Waterloo – primarily because it featured both Agnetha and Frida so prominently.

MY MAMA SAID (B Andersson / B Ulvaeus)
Nice little intro to this one and a clever little bit of jazz playing from Janne Schaffer. With the dual vocals from the girls this was as good a song as any to show how good the band were without Benny and Bjorns singing contributions. One of the more listenable tracks on the album.

DANCE (WHILE THE MUSIC STILL GOES ON)
(B Andersson / B Ulvaeus)
Actually a very pleasant number to listen to years on. Although a little slower than some of ABBA's more popular numbers this works very well.

HONEY HONEY (B Andersson / B Ulvaeus)
At less than three minutes long this again is a perfect pop song. Yet another example of what a good thing the band were onto by not letting the men sing! They do in this one but the song would have been so much better had they not!

Chosen by the band as the follow up single to Waterloo it did scale the charts in several territories. The powers that be in the UK however decided to avoid this one as the main follow up single and tried once again with Ring, Ring. Ring, Ring did chart but not as high as the cover by Sweet Dreams of Honey Honey. Still, Benny and Björn, the writers would have been happy either way no doubt!

WATCH OUT (B Andersson / B Ulvaeus)
For ABBA this is certainly a weird one and quite refreshingly too! The song was released as the B-side to Waterloo. Glam Rock was big in 1974 so who can blame ABBA for having a crack at it! Today it's an amusing one to listen to.

WHAT ABOUT LIVINGSTONE (B Andersson / B Ulvaeus)
Another catchy Benny and Björn number. Nothing outstanding but a nice little bit of pop all the same.

GONNA SING YOU MY LOVESONG (B Andersson / B Ulvaeus)
Beautiful guitar playing in this song and gentle piano but the song never really seems to get there. It's almost as if it was never really finished despite the keyboard layers. Nice ending as well. It's not a horrible song however and quite frankly would make a great song for another female artist to cover given the right arrangement.

SUZY-HANG-AROUND (B Andersson / B Ulvaeus)
Sounding just like Mr Tambourine Man for the intro, the song is another nice piece by ABBA. A little different than their (to date) usual offerings this song would not have been out of place on any number of albums by top-selling American female artists of the time. Interestingly it featured Benny on lead vocals! Nice bass playing in this one as well.

BONUS TRACKS:

RING, RING (US Re-mix) (B Andersson / S Anderson / B Ulvaeus / N Sedaka / P Cody)
It's always the Yanks isn't it! We must have a 'different' mix! – why? Are American ears that different? Nonetheless this was requested by the US record company exec's and duly produced. Not too far removed from the original it is included as a bonus track – quite right too!

WATERLOO (Swedish Version) *(B Andersson / S Anderson / B Ulvaeus)*
Again not as good as the original English version – it is fun to hear though – and even more fun to watch if you have the DVD clip of this one. It just goes to show a good tune is a good tune no matter what language it's sung in.

HONEY, HONEY (Swedish Version) *(B Andersson / S Anderson / B Ulvaeus)*
Not a lot different quite frankly than the English version and after a few drinks I defy anyone to be able to tell the difference. Nice as a bonus track, especially if you can sing in Swedish.

WATERLOO (German Version) *(B Andersson / S Anderson / B Ulvaeus)*
Not on the original 1991 CD re-master. Sound and vision version only. Far better in English! …or even Swedish for that matter. Some languages just do not translate too well to music and German is definitely one of them. Nice try though and no doubt it sorted a few more million sales out for the band. Now if only a German heavy metal band would try and cover this one. In German!

WATERLOO (French Version) *(B Andersson / S Anderson / B Ulvaeus)*
Not on the original 1991 CD re-master. Sound and vision version only. In French, if this had actually been about the battle of Waterloo it would have really stabbed at French pride. It isn't however, mind you it sounds nearly as bad in French as it does in German. Enough said.

BONUS DVD TRACKS ON SOUND AND VISION RELEASE:

WATERLOO (Eurovision Song contest – BBC recording)
A great number and so much fun to hear it with the pictures. Classic pop delivered in classic seventies fashion. Although mimed to the original backing track (with horns and vocals live of course!) A good addition as a bonus track.

WATERLOO (Melodifestivalen, Swedish Televison)
Sung in Swedish and delivered in hot pants by Agnetha. Who was ever going to complain about this one! This is actually a live performance which is nice too.

HONEY, HONEY (Star Parade, ZDF)
Not live but a mimed performance, worth it nonetheless for the great getup the band are decked out in. Wonderful stuff!

HASTA MANANA (Senoras Y Senores, RTVE)
Mimed for Spanish TV this one is more than a laugh and a half to see in action!

ABBA
Originally released 21st April 1975.
Sweden: Polar Music POLS262,
UK: Epic EPC 80835, 7th June 1975.
CD re-master, 2001: Polar Music 549 952-2.
Sound and Vision release, 2004: Polar 0602498107287-features one audio disc and one separate DVD.

After two albums the co-operative that had started calling themselves Björn & Benny, Agnetha & Frida for the Ring Ring album then mutated to ABBA for the Eurovision song contest and then the release of the Waterloo album they decided to really cement the acronym as their professional monicker. ABBA's self titled third album to many is regarded as the first fully fledged album from the members as a full blown band. Either way it was the start of the real pop revolution as far as album releases were concerned for the band. The album sold by the truckload, as did the singles lifted from it. Little did they know that this was just the beginning!

MAMMA MIA (B Andersson / S Anderson / B Ulvaeus)
One of the most well known tracks by Abba and the one that has spawned a musical that runs in several cities around the planet. Love or hate this song once you listen to it you will be humming it for a long time! Piano and marimba feature prominently and the guitar playing is pretty damn good too. Mama Mia was the second UK number one for the group (Waterloo was the first). Interestingly Mamma Mia was not slated for a single release at all but it was the call of the Australian marketing gurus that ensured its release. It shot to number one in Australia then all over the world. Although not as strong musically as several other tracks on the album no one can doubt its bubble gum appeal and obvious success.

ABBA receiving an ovation from the crowd at the end of one of their live shows

HEY, HEY HELEN *(B Andersson / B Ulvaeus)*

A strong vocal presentation from the girls this is a 'real' album track. Not one that would have been a hugely successful single but it's more than acceptable in the context of the album.

TROPICAL LOVELAND *(B Andersson / S Anderson / B Ulvaeus)*

Obviously trying to capture that Caribbean and Island spirit this one really does fall short of the mark. Not a bad song perse and the girls' vocals are nice but it is certainly nothing special.

SOS *(B Andersson / S Anderson / B Ulvaeus)*

Quite possibly the best ABBA song ever! This one has everything in it that was good about the band. Wonderful lyrics, fantastic hook and cool melody. Bands all over the world wish for songs such as this. ABBA were always a band that heavier bands could have (and should have) looked to for clever songs to cover. One such band, Nazareth (hit makers in their own right) did cover this track – with stunningly good results. To date the recording still resides in the vaults however. It is a perfect example of how good writers Benny, Björn and Stig could be. Classic seventies pop song writing at its very best.

MAN IN THE MIDDLE (B Andersson / B Ulvaeus)
One might be forgiven for not knowing this was ABBA on the first hearing. Nice electric piano and guitar playing. One of the better songs ABBA has ever attempted using both the male and female vocal. A nice album track.

BANG-A-BOOMERANG (B Andersson / S Anderson / B Ulvaeus)
A classic track from the album and one that had a great feel to it way back when! And it still sounds good today even if it is full of rather benign lyrics. Another catchy number that you won't be able to get out of your head – even after one listen!

Not released as a single in countries that usually contributed to the huge sales the track was originally included as (good) album filler by Benny and Björn. Interestingly it was a Benny/Björn number that they had written several years earlier and it was then used as a launch pad for Polar Music artists Svenne and Lotta for an entry into the Eurovision song contest. They came third and consequently did not repeat ABBA's success of the previous year.

I DO, I DO, I DO, I DO, I DO (B Andersson / S Anderson / B Ulvaeus)
Another of those classic girlie numbers that this band always did so well. The music itself does retain a slight latin feel and in years gone by I have even heard this one blasted out by scores of professional Mariachi players in El Salvador and other Central American countries! Number one in Australia and being constantly played at weddings presumably as the brides were holding the groom by the scruff of the neck, ankles or some other extremity of their body.

ROCK ME (B Andersson / B Ulvaeus)
Björn's attempt at copying Noddy Holder. Slade had been huge just a few years earlier and this was an obvious nod in their direction. ABBA-rized of course. Certainly a good pop song that might well have worked with Agnetha or Frida taking the lead. Fun addition to the album all the same.

INTERMEZZO NO. 1 (B Andersson / B Ulvaeus)
For those that thought ABBA were just a bunch of singles artists and couldn't write anything more than that, this must have been a real upsetter. It's a very clever take on 'hits' from the classical era and it's a shame they never really did more stuff like this.

I'VE BEEN WAITING FOR YOU (B Andersson / S Anderson / B Ulvaeus)

A lovely ballad that even has a guitar break that sounds reminiscent of Steve Howe of Yes from their Relayer album released a year earlier. Classic singing from Agnetha this wonderful number was a top ten hit downunder in little old New Zealand.

SO LONG (B Andersson / B Ulvaeus)

Another song that could easily have come from the pen of Roy Wood (Wizzard). Waterloo was another of course. The similarity of these two songs to the material Wood was releasing in 1972 and 1973 is quite striking. This one by ABBA is a great little rock and roller.

BONUS TRACKS:
CRAZY WORLD (B Andersson / B Ulvaeus)

Rather gentle number with a very wimpy sounding lead vocal from Björn. The tune would probably have worked a lot better had one of the girls worked their magic on it. The probable reason for not doing so was the subject matter of the song which was directed from a man to a woman. Originally recorded for these album sessions it was discarded and later picked up and worked on again during the Arrival sessions. It made its vinyl debut as the B-side to Money, Money, Money in 1976. Nice addition for those in collectorville however.

PICK A BALE OF COTTON / ON TOP OF OLD SMOKEY / MIDNIGHT SPECIAL

(Trad. Arrangement - B Andersson / B Ulvaeus)

Recorded not long after the ABBA album sessions for a German charity album. With the proceeds going to a good cause, a cancer fund. The songs were all out of copyright and therefore in the public domain which meant the proceeds would not be tied up with needless claims for the charities' operations and subsequent claim on funds. The song was later re-mixed and issued as the B-side to Summer Night City from the Voulez-Vous sessions. Not a classic that's for sure and really little more than a curio it does deserve a place as a bonus track. Interestingly it was the only material recorded by ABBA that was not self penned.

ARRIVAL

Originally released 11th October 1976.
Sweden: Polar Music POLS272,
UK: Epic EPC 86018, 5th November 1976.
CD re-master, 2001: Polar Music 549 953-2. Sound and Vision release, 2004: Polar 981 073-3 - features one audio disc and one separate DVD.

Album number four and the band had certainly arrived in no uncertain terms. The previous self titled album and the singles lifted from it had shifted large numbers of units the world over. The band were topping the charts and with that came fame and plenty of money. The outfits became more outrageous and 1976 was certainly a period when the members looked young, vibrant and sexy. Not many teenage boys from 1976 will ever forget the sight of the girls in their tight white boiler suits. Some sights live on forever!

The album is once again a clever mix of ballads and pop and the cover is a memorable one from that mid seventies period. The band's next album was to take them to even higher heights and the helicopter image was just the start of their high-flying period.

WHEN I KISSED THE TEACHER *(B Andersson / B Ulvaeus)*
ABBA pop at its best again. A lovely mix of the girls' vocals especially Agnetha's. A simple almost acoustic track that works ever so well.

DANCING QUEEN *(B Andersson / S Anderson / B Ulvaeus)*
An instant dance classic that was to be the band's one and only number one in the US. It charted all over the world and became one of the band's signature tunes. If there is ever a track that is instantly recognisable as ABBA this has got to be it. The song is wonderfully constructed pop that was first made famous when played just prior to the wedding of the Swedish King and his bride to be in the summer of 1976.

MY LOVE, MY LOVE *(B Andersson / B Ulvaeus)*

A rather lovely piece. Not single material for sure but a nice addition to the album and it's a track that has stood the test of time far better than some of the romping singles. Sung by the queen of heart-break Agnetha. Allegedly inspired by British pop outfit 10CC. One listen and you can certainly tell why.

DUM DUM DIDDLE *(B Andersson / B Ulvaeus)*

The title says it all as far as the lyrics are concerned. The track however is a pleasant enough piece of pop.

KNOWING ME, KNOWING YOU *(B Andersson / S Anderson / B Ulvaeus)*

Another classic seventies piece of heartbreak and this one has a fair chance of claiming the crown for exactly that subject. As teenagers we would all have related to this at some time or another even if one didn't like the song. The girlfriends we had dumped or whom had dumped us all loved this one! Although the lyrics point to an older set not many of us would have recognised or acknowledged that fact at the time. This became a UK number one.

MONEY, MONEY, MONEY *(B Andersson / B Ulvaeus)*

Frida sang this one and her spin on the subject and sound are truly exceptional. The musicianship is exceptional as usual and the track has beome an all time favourite the world over. It is certainly a highlight from the Arrival album and it became the third single to be lifted from the album. The single reached number one in Australia, New Zealand, Mexico and Holland just to name a few countries.

THAT'S ME *(B Andersson / S Anderson / B Ulvaeus)*

Released as the B-side to Dancing Queen (except in Japan where it was an A-side!). The song has a lovely vocal sound with backing vocals that are not unlike Queen from the same period.

WHY DID IT HAVE TO BE ME *(B Andersson / B Ulvaeus)*

Björn lead vocal on this one and actually it's not too bad. The only one on the album in fact. The track was recorded initially with the feel laid down here, then re-recorded (as Happy Hawaii) then it went through more interpretation before the writing team reverted to the original feel. Not a classic but an acceptable album track.

TIGER (B Andersson / B Ulvaeus)

For ABBA, a reasonably rocky little number. Great title and the track romps along well. Interestingly a band called Survivor had a major hit with Eye Of The Tiger several years later. The track is not completely disimimilier when one breaks it down and if a heavy version had been done of this it could well have screamed up the charts.

ARRIVAL (B Andersson / S Anderson / B Ulvaeus)

Some great moog and mellotron work on this one from Benny. Heavily influenced by Swedish folk music which Benny loved so much. Some say this should never have appeared on an ABBA album. Personally I think it is one of the nicest pieces of music they ever recorded. A lovely way to end the album.

BONUS TRACKS:

FERNANDO (B Andersson / S Anderson / B Ulvaeus)

Not released on the album (except in New Zealand and Australia) the track was released as a highly successful single. Later this was included as an essential track on the various Best Ofs. The track itself has a lovely latino lilt and it works well showing the gentle downbeat side of ABBA.

HAPPY HAWAII (B Andersson / S Anderson / B Ulvaeus)

Released as the B-side of Knowing Me, Knowing You the track was actually a re-working of Why Did It Have To Be Me and in some ways this version is far more ABBA-esque attempt. A nice addition for the re-master.

THE ALBUM

Originally released 12th December 1978.
Sweden: Polar Music POLS282
UK: Epic EPC 86052, 13th January 1978.
CD re-master, 2001: Polar Music 549 954-2

The Album was the point where ABBA really started to mature musically. Previously only really recognised for short pop songs Benny and Björn were keen to try and expand their horizons. This they certainly started to do in earlier albums (Intermezzo No. 1 being a good example), however the albums were still often a bit of a mish-mash of songs, albeit good ones.

EAGLE *(B Andersson / B Ulvaeus)*

An unusual way for ABBA to start an album. The song however is arguably one of the best compositions they have ever laid down to tape. Running in at nearly six minutes it's also one of the longest. The track features wonderful guitar playing and nice touches of synth. The girls' dual vocal is exceptionally good. Eagle is a song that really has not dated and in fact sounds better today than ever before. It's a shame ABBA did not record a lot more material like this. Top class this one.

TAKE A CHANCE ON ME *(B Andersson / B Ulvaeus)*

Allegedly inspired from an idea Björn had while running. Actually the sound of his feet hitting the pavement. He and Benny had certainly not lost the ability to pen a clever pop song from a normal fact of his daily life. The song was the second single to be lifted from The Album and reached number one in the UK, number three in the US and it also topped the charts in many other territories. A good fun track to listen to even today... especially while... er... running!

ONE MAN, ONE WOMAN *(B Andersson / B Ulvaeus)*

Sung by Frida the song was probably based around the troubles Agnetha and

ABBA just before the band broke up

Björn were having in their private life. The song is actually quite a heart rending little gem and it really shows what a strong voice Frida had.

THE NAME OF THE GAME (B Andersson / S Anderson / B Ulvaeus)
Released as the first single from the album it quickly shot to number one. A simple number that makes especially good use of both Agnetha and Frida's vocals.

MOVE ON (B Andersson / S Anderson / B Ulvaeus)
With clever use of Peruvian pan pipes this is probably the best thing about this track. Its not a bad one and the use of Björn's talking vocal is amusing. The girls' vocals are superb of course. The track overall is little more than good album filler however.

HOLE IN YOUR SOUL (B Andersson / B Ulvaeus)
ABBA doing a rock 'n' roll number and this one is an exceptionally good one. Simple but very effective its use of Benny and Björn's vocal intermixed with Agnetha and Frida works very well. The synthesiser work is very good too. A great live track.

THE GIRL WITH GOLDEN HAIR:
3 SCENES FROM A MINI MUSICAL

The mini musical was performed live during the 1977 Australian and European tour. The studio versions were included on The Album. This almost certainly sowed the seed for what Benny and Björn would do years after ABBA's split in the form of Mamma Mia.

THANK YOU FOR THE MUSIC *(B Andersson / B Ulvaeus)*

Very much a music hall style and Agnetha's vocal is superb. This has remained a favourite with fans since its inception during the 1977 tour, quite possibly because it captures the feel of days gone by ever so well.

I WONDER (DEPARTURE) *(B Andersson / S Anderson / B Ulvaeus)*

Second song of the trio and the one that really is about that girl with the golden hair. Superb singing by Frida, quite possibly it was so enigmatic because she may have been expressing her own feelings for real. Superb stuff for a musical.

I'M A MARIONETTE *(B Andersson / B Ulvaeus)*

Certainly one of the more dramatic songs in ABBA's canon. Superbly played throughout I'm A Marionette is actually quite a masterpiece. Wonderful subtle guitar playing in this one as well. The intro could easily have come from any number of classic progressive rock bands around at the time. In fact the style and feel is something many of them quite possibly strived for without ever achieving anything as good as this one.

BONUS TRACKS:
THANK YOU FOR THE MUSIC
(Doris Day version) *(B Andersson / B Ulvaeus)*

This is the first version of Thank You For The Music and as such is more like a work in progress recording. It lacks the synth and keyboard fills and as such has not been 'ABBA-rized'. Not a classic version and certainly the best place for this version is as a bonus track. At least now we can programme out the ones we don't like!

VOULEZ-VOUS

Originally released 23rd April 1979.
Sweden: Polar Music POLS292,
UK: Epic EPC 86086, 27th April 1979.
CD re-master, 2001: Polar Music 549 955-2.

Voulez-Vous was the first album recorded in the band's own Polar Studios. A luxury they had wanted for a long time. Metronome was their favourite place of work but they could not guarantee unlimited use of the place so to have their own wonderfully kitted out studio was a sensible luxury.

Two relatively musical genres were in full swing in 1978. One was punk, the other disco and it didn't take a rocket scientist to work out which genre was going to be an obvious choice for ABBA, the kings and queens of pop to latch on to. One can't imagine ABBA as punk artists! It might have been quite something to hear thrashing guitars, no keyboards and the girls (safety pins in noses etc...) screeching out punk anthems with an ABBA twist!

Sessions were started in March 1978 in alternate studios before the band moved into Polar. Problems abounded however; Benny and Björn found it hard to find inspiration in the current climate (maybe they should have spun a couple of those old punk numbers on the turntable!) and Agnetha and Björn were going through a divorce. Interestingly, this may have made for a better album; plenty of heart rending material being penned by the band and the previous tensions being moved to one side. At least for a while. In fact it is quite a credit to all concerned that the band kept functioning the way they did through such traumatic events. On the other hand, Benny and Frida finally got married. The contrast couldn't be more different for all concerned. The album sold many millions of course.

AS GOOD AS NEW (B Andersson / B Ulvaeus)

This Agnetha led track reached number one in Mexico of all places and it wasn't even sung in Spanish! A cool little pop number that may well be Agnetha voicing her ideas about her divorce. Clever bits of guitar on this one too.

VOULEZ-VOUS (B Andersson / B Ulvaeus)

During a trip to the Bahamas for writing inspiration as much as holiday Benny and Björn stopped in nearby Miami and laid down the backing track for this one in Criteria Studios (at the time famous for everyone from the Bee Gees through to the then recently deceased Tommy Bolin). Voulez-Vous was more than a little heavily disco tinged. This was the third single lifted from the album and remains a favourite even today.

I HAVE A DREAM (B Andersson / B Ulvaeus)

The fourth and final single from the album, this one reached number two in the UK. A wonderful vocal from Frida and a children's choir really make this quite a lovely little number. Certainly a song that could be included in any decent musical and the girls love this one!

ANGELEYES (B Andersson / B Ulvaeus)

In the UK this song was released as a double A-side (with Voulez-Vous). It reached number three. With Agnetha and Frida both taking lead vocals the song was highly typical of the ABBA of old.

THE KING LOST HIS CROWN (B Andersson / B Ulvaeus)

An excellent album track but not one that was ever likely to make a brilliant single. Sung by Frida this is still a quaint one to hear today.

DOES YOUR MOTHER KNOW (B Andersson / B Ulvaeus)

The second single from the album and this time sung by Björn and it reached the top five in a number of countries. Had the girls taken the lead with this one it is almost certain they would have topped the charts all over the world as the song is extremely catchy. Not just a little bit Bee Gees influenced, but hey, they were all the rage at the time. Simple but good.

IF IT WASN'T FOR THE NIGHT (B Andersson / B Ulvaeus)

A rather gentle track and one that really siginified the period for ABBA.

Gentle disco rhythm that makes for a sensible album track. Nothing outstanding but its not terrible either.

CHIQUITITA (B Andersson / B Ulvaeus)

One of the most popular Abba songs sung by Agnetha. It was also the first single to be lifted from the album. The band played this live at a benefit concert in New York with all future revenue from publishing the song being donated to UNICEF. With a latin flavour this has always been popular with latin girls the world over. Even today this will make them all bleary eyed when they hear it on the radio.

LOVERS (LIVE A LITTLE LONGER) (B Andersson / B Ulvaeus)

With Frida singing that the more sex you get the longer you live how could one resist this track! Quite an unusual style for ABBA but it does work very well. Certainly a song that has stood the test of time better than many others from ABBA's canon.

KISSES OF FIRE (B Andersson / B Ulvaeus)

A mixture of the maturity in music ABBA was discovering and pure pop, this one ends the album quite nicely. Agnetha's vocal is as strong as ever and the slightly rocky feel at times give this song a nice edge.

BONUS TRACKS:

SUMMER NIGHT CITY (B Andersson / B Ulvaeus)

Originally slated for inclusion on the album but not included on the initial release Summer Night City was released as a single. Featuring lead vocals from all of the band members it has a very cool feel to it. The girls' vocals really give it the lift however. It is a welcome addition as a bonus track on the album it should have been on in the first place.

LOVELIGHT (B Andersson / B Ulvaeus)

Previously issued as the B-side to the Chiquitita single Lovelight was a Voulez-Vous album out-take that never quite made the grade.

GIMME! GIMME! GIMME! (A MAN AFTER MIDNIGHT) (B Andersson / B Ulvaeus)

Certainly one of the best rock-pop-disco combinations of all time. Benny and

Björn really created a great pop song with this one. Agnetha delivers another soaring vocal to good effect. The single was released just prior to the US tour of 1979 and sold by the truckload. Literally.

SUPER TROUPER

Originally released 3rd November 1980.
Sweden: Polar Music POLS322,
UK: Epic EPC 10022, 21st November 1980
CD re-master, 2001: Polar Music 549 956-2

Again Recorded in Stockholm at Polar Music studios Super Trouper was probably the most polished ABBA album recorded at that point. There are several highlights on the album and the overall feel is quite balanced. Overall a good album if not quite as adventurous as some previous efforts. This album was a real turning point for the band both in recording and the general direction of the band. Little did they realise it at the time but they only had one more studio album in them after Super Trouper. They also stopped touring the world (as far as concerts were concerned anyway). They had certainly reached a peak and maybe the stress of touring, strained relationships within the band and the fact they actually had so much money accumulated they really never had to work again may have contributed to the ultimate completion of their recording career soon after this.

SUPER TROUPER *(B Andersson / B Ulvaeus)*
Pure pop this one, pure ABBA too. This one was the second single to be lifted from the album and it charted well all over the world. Super Trouper was actually inspired and named from the massive stage spotlights used on tour.

THE WINNER TAKES IT ALL *(B Andersson / B Ulvaeus)*
Quite possibly one of the best songs ABBA ever recorded. The lyrics were penned by Björn in the wake of his divorce from Agnetha and although he has

said it is not entirely personal it is obvious it comes from the heart. Anyone who has been divorced will relate to this one in no uncertain terms. Maybe, however it should have been re-titled There Are No Winners In It All!

ON AND ON AND ON (B Andersson / B Ulvaeus)

Another clever pop/rock song that has a definite seventies appeal. It is actually quite typical of a number of other songs that were kicking around at the same time and it must be no coincidence that Benny and Björn may have heard something similer on the radio and created a variation on a theme. It actually works very well and one wonders what this would sound like rocked up somewhat.

ANDANTE, ANDANTE (B Andersson / B Ulvaeus)

A nice Frida sung ballad that was more than adequate as an album track. It is doubtful it would ever have done much business as a single.

ME AND I (B Andersson / B Ulvaeus)

Another synthesised pop ditty with the lead sung by Frida. Listen to this one and you can certainly tell where ABBA's countrymen Europe took some inspiration from for their hit single The Final Countdown.

HAPPY NEW YEAR (B Andersson / B Ulvaeus)

This one was sung by Agnetha. Nice enough number although it does go on a bit too long. It was considered as a single at one point.

OUR LAST SUMMER (B Andersson / B Ulvaeus)

Lyrics penned by Björn about a summer adventure he had as a teenager. We've all been there I guess! Sung beautifully by Frida. Nice if slightly out of place guitar solo in the middle of the song.

THE PIPER (B Andersson / B Ulvaeus)

Apparently inspired by Stephen King's The Stand the music has a lovely 'King Arthur' feel to it. Actually a very good song and sung beautifully by the girls. This is something the band could have (and should have) made a great deal more of. It certainly precedes what former Deep Purple guitarist Richie Blackmore and Candice Night started recording and releasing to great success in the late nineties.

LAY ALL YOUR LOVE ON ME *(B Andersson / B Ulvaeus)*
One of the more memorable tracks from the ABBA canon. Released in the UK as a 12 inch single it hit the top ten quickly and easily. This was a song that with its disco beat and simple spacey feel probably would have done extremely well in the US had it been pushed. It has certainly stood the test of time well, making for an easy track to listen to today. Good relaxing stuff.

THE WAY OLD FRIENDS DO *(B Andersson / B Ulvaeus)*
Recorded live in November 1979 during six nights at Wembley Arena in London this is a take on Auld Lang Syne. Benny on accordian gives this a nice feel. If you purchase the ABBA In Concert DVD you can even see the band in full swing with this one. Timeless song and a clever choice to end an album with.

BONUS TRACKS:

ELAINE *(B Andersson / B Ulvaeus)*
Originally to be included on the album it was omitted and then used as the B-side to The Winner Takes It All. Interesting synth feel and sounds but one can see why it was omitted as an album track. Nice addition here however.

PUT ON YOUR WHITE SOMBRERO *(B Andersson / B Ulvaeus)*
One could say this is actually quite a good song. I'm not going to however. One can see why this remained unreleased for fourteen odd years. Granted it's not terrible and it might have appealed to the Latin market in 1980 but it certainly would not have done much business in ABBA's usual big-time markets. It's well played but it does lack that usual top-shelf feel ABBA could so often attain. The best place for this track is here as a bonus track on CD or on your ipod where it can be programmed out if necessary.

THE VISITORS

Originally released 30th November 1981.
Sweden: Polar Music POLS342,
UK: Epic EPC 10032, 11th December 1981.
CD re-master, 2001: Polar Music 549 957-2

The final album from the fab two plus two! The Visitors hit the streets in late 1981 and it was doubtful this was ever planned as a final album. The band did re-enter the studio in August 1982 to record more songs and then decided to take a break to allow Benny and Björn to concentrate on their planned musical Chess with Tim Rice. The girls planned to record solo albums. However once the music for Chess had been recorded and then staged in London in 1986 it seemed all impetus to re-group and record had disappeared. The Visitors therefore became the final vinyl offering in long player format from the band. The extra tracks recorded in the August of 1982 have sensibly been added as bonus tracks to the final CD re-master.

Listening to the album years later it probably stands the test of time better than any other album from the band. It may not have sold as well as the earlier albums but it certainly holds together very well as an album.

THE VISITORS *(B Andersson / B Ulvaeus)*
Vocally this must be one of the best songs Frida sang lead on. The mix of heavy synths and keyboards just adds to the flavour wonderfully. Based around the paranoia that abounded in the early eighties regarding the Soviet Bloc the lyrical content is actually very mature for ABBA. Cool song that really should have been a single had the band taken a little risk.

HEAD OVER HEELS *(B Andersson / B Ulvaeus)*
Second track in and Agnetha is on top form with a brilliant tune. Released as the second single from the album it only reached number 25. Many critics have slated this tune, however if one gives it a good listen they will find a great tune

and a mature approach to the song in general. Bottom line is ABBA were writing better more fulfilling songs and maybe the audiences were just not ready to accept that. Good effort nonetheless.

WHEN ALL IS SAID AND DONE (B Andersson / B Ulvaeus)
Another song about the internal break-ups, this time between Benny and Frida. Frida herself has said she put her heart and soul into the song and you can certainly hear the emotion in her valiant and more than capable attempt. The song itself has a simple beat that works very well. Released as a single in several territories.

SOLDIERS (B Andersson / B Ulvaeus)
Lyrically a little different than the norm and musically quite a lot different from the usual things ABBA attempted. The track does show a maturity and as with several other tracks on The Visitors album it displays a need to deal with problems in the world as perceived in the early eighties in Europe. All in all a nice number, shame there weren't more like this one.

I LET THE MUSIC SPEAK (B Andersson / B Ulvaeus)
Another quite long tune (for ABBA at least!) that has a wonderful vocal performance from Frida. Not a typical ABBA piece and one that certainly shows the direction Benny and Bjorn seemed to be heading; musicals. This track was a perfect example to display what they could deliver. A good album track.

ONE OF US (B Andersson / B Ulvaeus)
Released as a single and peaking at number five, One Of Us was the last real hit ABBA were to have. Fantastic sound and beautiful vocals from Agnetha. Full of heart rending stories of break-ups it was just what the fans wanted.

TWO FOR THE PRICE OF ONE (B Andersson / B Ulvaeus)
Another one that had this been sung by one of the girls rather than Björn it would have had a chance of being a big hit. Not that one can criticise the writer for wanting to sing a few of his songs. After all he had enough of them!

SLIPPING THROUGH MY FINGERS (B Andersson / B Ulvaeus)
Written by Björn about his young daughter leaving for school it was sung by Agnetha who has said it was the most enjoyable song for her to record on the

album. A nice song that anyone with children will relate to – and that is the secret to much of ABBA's success. Their ability to record songs that could mean so much to people.

LIKE AN ANGEL PASSING THROUGH MY ROOM
(B Andersson / B Ulvaeus)

A very beautiful song with Frida delivering the vocal. The ticking clock was a nice touch and the general feel gives the original album a lovely end. Time passed and all that. A good end to a good album.

BONUS TRACKS:
SHOULD I LAUGH OR CRY *(B Andersson / B Ulvaeus)*

Originally slated for inclusion on the album this track eventually ended up as the B-side to One Of Us. Not a bad number and it certainly made a more than adequate B-side.

THE DAY BEFORE YOU CAME *(B Andersson / B Ulvaeus)*

One of the very last ABBA recordings this nearly six minute mini epic did hit the top 5 in a number of territories. In the UK however it didn't even break the top 30. The song itself is a very good one and certainly something that must have taught Annie Lennox a few things. The new romantic feel is ever present and beautifully sung by Agnetha. It is a song that certainly would have been perfect to cover regardless of whether people bought this track. There is no doubting Björn and Benny could write great tunes. This was one of the lost ABBA classics. Good inclusion as a bonus track.

CASSANDRA *(B Andersson / B Ulvaeus)*

One of the last recordings ever made by ABBA. Sung by Frida this album-worthy track ended up as the B-side to The Day Before You Came single purely because there was not an album to include it on.

UNDER ATTACK *(B Andersson / B Ulvaeus)*

The final single by ABBA and although the song is okay it wasn't exactly the best choice for a single. Reaching only number 26 in the UK kind of spoke volumes at the time as well. It may well have been their waning in the (UK) charts that encouraged the band to pack it in while they were ahead. Whatever the reason they left a fantastic legacy of extremely well constructed and performed pop music.

ABBA LIVE

Originally released 18th August 1986-Both LP and CD versions. Sweden: Polar Music POLS412 and POLCD412, UK: Polydor 829 951-2, 9th April 1992.

When work started on ABBA – The Album plans were in place to make it a double album with one disk featuring studio works and the other live material from recent live recordings. This plan was shelved until another plan was hatched to release the 1979 Wembley recordings. This was quashed by the band as they believed it was always better to just hear their studio versions. Several live tracks did hits the streets from various sources via flexi disc releases, compilations and the like. However it wasn't until four years after the last studio recordings that the band agreed to release live material. They didn't relish returning to the studio for a fully fledged studio project and with a new royalty deal and Polar Music breathing down their necks to produce some sort of release, suitable live material was sanctioned.

Three concert sources were used; Australia 1977, Wembley, London, UK 1979 and Swedish Television in studio concert from 1981.

The recordings were (sadly) duly doctored and edited to make it sound as one concert, in the process losing much of the live essence. The mix and mastering is also rather appalling, certainly a candidate for a good re-master job or better still a clever 5.1 surround sound job done on it! That would make it worth buying. That aside these are the only official live recordings available on CD by ABBA to date. On DVD, well that's a different story.

Dancing Queen *(B Andersson / S Anderson / B Ulvaeus)*
Recorded Wembley Arena, November 1979. Original studio version appeared on Arrival.

Take A Chance On Me *(B Andersson / B Ulvaeus)*

Recorded Wembley Arena, November 1979. Original studio version appeared on ABBA – The Album.

I Have A Dream *(B Andersson / B Ulvaeus)*

Recorded Wembley Arena, November 1979. Original studio version appeared on Voulez-Vous.

Does Your Mother Know *(B Andersson / B Ulvaeus)*

Recorded Wembley Arena, November 1979. Original studio version appeared on Voulez-Vous.

Chiquitita *(B Andersson / B Ulvaeus)*

Recorded Wembley Arena, November 1979. Original studio version appeared on Voulez-Vous.

Thank You For The Music *(B Andersson / B Ulvaeus)*

Recorded Wembley Arena, November 1979. Original studio version appeared on ABBA – The Album.

Two For The Price Of One *(B Andersson / B Ulvaeus)*

Recorded by Swedish TV for the Dick Cavett meets ABBA TV special 1981. Original studio version appeared on The Visitors.

Fernando *(B Andersson / S Anderson / B Ulvaeus)*

Recorded in Australia during the 1977 world tour. Original studio version appeared on the New Zealand and Australian versions of Arrival. Elsewhere it was only released as a single.

Gimme! Gimme! Gimme! (A Man After Midnight) *(B Andersson / B Ulvaeus)*

Recorded by Swedish TV for the Dick Cavett meets ABBA TV special 1981. Original studio version was originally only released as a single.

Super Trouper *(B Andersson / B Ulvaeus)*

Recorded by Swedish TV for the Dick Cavett meets ABBA TV special 1981. Original studio version appeared on Super Trouper.

Waterloo *(B Andersson / S Anderson / B Ulvaeus)*

Recorded Wembley Arena, November 1979. Original studio version appeared on Waterloo.

BONUS TRACKS FOR CD VERSION:

Money, Money, Money *(B Andersson / B Ulvaeus)*

Recorded in Australia during the 1977 world tour. Original studio version appeared on Arrival

The Name Of The Game *(B Andersson / S Anderson / B Ulvaeus)*

Eagle *(B Andersson / B Ulvaeus)*

Recorded Wembley Arena, November 1979. Original studio versions for both appeared on ABBA – The Album.

On And On And On *(B Andersson / B Ulvaeus)*

Recorded by Swedish TV for the Dick Cavett meets ABBA TV special 1981. Original studio version appeared on Super Trouper.

HABLAR ESPANOL! GRACIAS POR LA MUSCIA

Originally released 23rd June 1980. Sweden: Septima SRLM1, UK: EPIC EOC 86123, 18th July 1980. CD re-master – none to date using the same title.

ABBA ORO – GRANDES EXITOS

Polar Music 543 129-2, 9th September 2002.

The 'lingua de Espanol' recordings or Spanish Language recordings have been released several times over in quite a number of territories over the years. It was not until the release of Grandes Exitos however that all of the Spanish sung or Spanish related tracks were released as one product. If you are into this kind of thing then it is this release that is the essential collection. The Spanish lyrics were translated / composed via a husband and wife team Buddy and Mary McCluskey from RCA Argentina who handled Polar releases in Latin America. The original album or variations on the album were released in many Latin countries charting highly in Spain and Argentina to name a few. It was also released in the UK and several other English speaking territories, selling acceptable numbers of units primarily on the back of the band's popularity at the time.

Gracias Por La Música *(B Andersson / B Ulvaeus / B & M McClusky)*
Spanish version of Thank You For The Music

Reina Danzante *(B Andersson / B Ulvaeus / S Anderson/ B & M McClusky)*
Spanish version of Dancing Queen. Later released under the name of La

Reina Del Baile

Al Andar *(B Andersson / B Ulvaeus / S Anderson / B & M McClusky)*

Spanish version of Move On

Dame! Dame! Dame! *(B Andersson / B Ulvaeus / B & M McClusky)*

Spanish version of Gimme! Gimme! Gimme! (A Man After Midnight)

Fernando *(B Andersson / B Ulvaeus / S Anderson / B & M McClusky)*

Spanish version of... well er... Fernando !

Estoy Soñando *(B Andersson / B Ulvaeus / B & M McClusky)*

Spanish version of I Have A Dream

Mamma Mia *(B Andersson / B Ulvaeus / S Anderson / B & M McClusky)*

Spanish version of ..wait for it! ..Mamma Mia

Hasta Mañana *(B Andersson / B Ulvaeus / S Anderson / B & M McClusky)*

Spanish version of Hasta Mañana. This was actually the first track Abba recorded with a Spanish feel.

Conociéndome, Conociéndote *(B Andersson / B Ulvaeus / B & M McClusky)*

Spanish version of Knowing Me, Knowing You

Chiquitita *(B Andersson / B Ulvaeus / B & M McClusky)*

Spanish version of the same song. This was the track that rocked up the charts to number one in Argentina and Mexico and really created the impetus for further releases of Spanish singles and then long players like this one.

NB: It should be noted that the track order on the original album releases varied somewhat and this trend continued with the CD versions. Bonus tracks were added for the latest CD version released in 2002.

BONUS TRACKS FOR CD VERSION:

Felicidad *(B Andersson / B Ulvaeus / B & M McClusky)*

Spanish version of Happy New Year

Adante Adante *(B Andersson / B Ulvaeus / B & M McClusky)*

Spanish version of Adante Adante !

Se Me Está Escapando *(B Andersson / B Ulvaeus / B & M McClusky)*

Spanish version of Slipping Through My Fingers

No Hay A Quien Culpar *(B Andersson / B Ulvaeus / B & M McClusky)*

Spanish version of When All Is Said And Done

Ring Ring *(B Andersson / B Ulvaeus / S Anderson / D Band)*

Spanish version of Se Me Esta Escapando

VIDEO AND DVD – THE STORY SO FAR

ABBA are certainly a band that have not been short of video and DVD releases although many are variations on a theme. This is an area where one could write a mountain of material but as many of them duplicate one another in many ways I am not about to even go there! Of the ones easily obtainable today there are a few of particular note:

ABBA – THE DEFINITIVE COLLECTION
(released on DVD in the UK on the 29th July 2002 – Polar Music 017 445-9)
Good collection of 35 videos released by ABBA over their career. These also include several Spanish sung videos as well. All have been digitally re-mastered (and are far better versions than some of the bonus tracks on the Sound And Vision series of the re-mastered CD and DVD double sets.

ABBA – IN CONCERT
(released on DVD in the UK on the 29th March 2004 – Polar Music 065 646-9)
One of the few places one can actually obtain reasonable live footage of the band. Recorded and filmed during their 1979 tour of the US and Europe the DVD version is not bad at all. The songs performed are Waterloo, Eagle, Take A Chance On Me, Voulez-Vous, Chiquitita, I Have A Dream, Gimme! Gimme! Gimme! (A Man After Midnight), Knowing Me, Knowing You, Summer Night City, Dancing Queen, Does Your Mother Know, Hole In Your Soul, Thank You For The Music, The Way Old Friends Do. There are also some very informative interviews from the film director, promoter and tour producer of the original shows and some interesting footage of the band backstage. There are also excellent picture galleries included.

Other DVDs of note but certainly not essential are:
SUPER TROUPERS – A re-worked version of The Winner Takes It All video with some up to date interviews with all band members.
THE LAST VIDEO – ABBA songs with clever puppets! Interesting and best watched while stoned.
ABBA GOLD – THE GREATEST HITS – Emulates the nearly 27 million seller ABBA Gold album – only you see them as well as hear them. Most of the video clips (all except two) are on The Definitive Collection.

ABBA – THE MOVIE – Interesting tour (with weak plot) movie of the band in action. When this is released on DVD (as it is not at the time of going to press) this may well be worth a spin as hopefully it will be packed with mind numbing extras!

COMPILATIONS:

Obviously compilations are a common occurrence for any successful band and this is certainly true of ABBA. In the world of CD releases however one stands out well above the other for the average listener; the ABBA Gold set. More ABBA Gold did add some interesting B-sides and the like and the recently double packed version is usually a good set to pick up for Christmas and birthday presents! For those who want an in depth listen but do not want to shell out for all the albums the box set Thank You For The Music (released in 1994 with a bunch of interesting extras) is as good as any. The four CD set (and book) are really quite good, however eleven years on and counting and it is about time a really comprehensive job was done on a bumper (make it 6 CDs!) long box set.

Just as an end note on ABBA compilations - to cover every compilation released worldwide would keep us writing for about 25 years!

Extra information: For anyone wanting to really research the releases of ABBA and its members from 7-inch singles, EPs through to bootlegs and CDs there are several good websites. Two some sites which seem to have good (sometimes) impartial information in their (legal release) discography sections are www.abbasite.com and www.abba-world.net

The sites are largely kept up to date and one will find almost everything ABBA on these or their linked sites. One of the best sites for information on the not so legal (and hence live) material including numerous bootlegs is www.abbaplaza.com This gives a lot of information and is reasonably well set out.

There are several good books on ABBA as well although these could do with an up to date biography covering all the ins and outs, controversial happenings and general information.

NB: It should be noted that the information regarding releases and release dates is as accurate as possible. As complete a picture as possible has been compiled regarding the main releases but I have no doubt there are items that may be missing. The descriptions of songs and performances are personal opinion only.
Robert M. Corich

CPSIA information can be obtained
at www.ICGtesting.com
Printed in the USA
LVHW101823150321
681555LV00046B/588

9 781906 783594